THE OFFICIAL
M.B.A.
HANDBOOK

Jim Fisk   Robert Barron
Harvard M.B.A. '82   Harvard M.B.A. '82

Photographs by Christopher W. Morrow

WALLABY

A Wallaby Book
Published by Simon & Schuster
New York

Designed by JUDY ALLAN (THE DESIGNING WOMAN)

WALLABY and colophon are registered trademarks of Simon & Schuster
First Wallaby Books printing May 1982
10 9 8 7 6 5 4 3 2 1

Manufactured in the United States of America

Printed and bound by Semline, Inc.

ISBN: 0-671-44358-5

ii

ACKNOWLEDGMENTS

Many people assisted in the development of *The Official M.B.A. Handbook*, directly and indirectly.

Our Harvard Business School professors taught us everything we know about business, as well as some of the material in this book.

John Dorfman, Mike Wilkins, Hugh Holmes, Barry Parr, and especially T. Grandon Gill contributed to several chapters. Michelle di Palo helped with graphics. Edward Porter, Stephen Dent, Steven Considine, and Susan McHugh generously offered their comments. Ken Proctor of the Harvard Coop graciously lent us props. Hester Kaplan helped greatly with research and permissions. Ellie Maguire drew storyboards. Bioengineering was by Deborah Trustman.

We are also very grateful to the Conant Modeling Agency, and to Larry Gerber, Kevin Gorman, Larry Henry, Hee-Jin Kim, Ed Nelson, Diana Olney, Vince Pearce, Frank Ruppen, Don Scales, Jane Schmeiser, Al Sexton, George Van Amson, and Linda Zwack, for letting their faces be shown in this book.

Finally, we would like to thank Gene Brissie and Jack Artenstein of Simon & Schuster for their guidance throughout the preparation and writing of this manual; we hereby grant them honorary M.B.A.'s.

To Linda, **wordmonger,** *for her patience;*
to our families;
and to an economic system that still has the ability
to laugh at itself.

CONTENTS

PART FIVE:
CAREER
MANAGEMENT

PART SIX:
HOW TO
KEEP SCORE,
*or "I founded my own
$10 million company,
but my ex-roommate's
the executive V.P. of
Exxon. Am I ahead?"*

CREDITS

"I've just graduated from the Stanford Business School and I'm a workaholic."

Introduction

AMERICANS DEVELOP A fascination with business success at an early age. One of the sweetest childhood memories we all share is that first day we managed to drive the kid next door out of a friendly game of Monopoly by putting together a small hotel chain on Boardwalk and Park Place. But recapturing that incomparable thrill is more elusive once we have graduated to the *real* game of business. It's a tough world out there: the stakes are high, the rules are strictly enforced, and the competition's a little tougher than when you were just playing against your younger brother. In today's business world, if you don't know fundamentals, like how to talk and how to look, as well as side issues like finance and marketing, you'll be lucky if your business career ever gets past "Go."

In the past decade the best-seller lists have been crammed with self-help books on how to get ahead in business: *Dress for Success, Looking Out for Number One, Games Your Mother Never Taught You,* among others. So many millions of copies of these

1

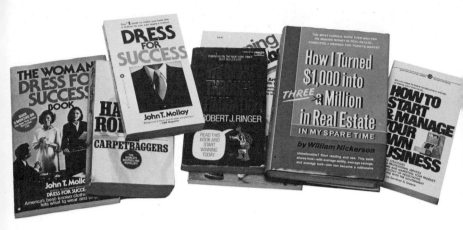

volumes have been sold to eager executives that it's hard to imagine how men like John D. Rockefeller and Andrew Carnegie managed to scrape together billion-dollar fortunes without knowing how to match their tie with their shirt or Win Through Intimidation. The fact is, most of these best-selling self-help authors never tasted real business success themselves until their books hit the big time, which says a lot for their ability to teach anything useful. The authors of this book, on the other hand, have spared no expense in trying to make this guide different. For one thing, we have each spent $25,000 and two years of study at the West Point of Capitalism to learn what it's *really* all about and to distill for you, in this book, the essentials of a Harvard Business School M.B.A. (Master of Business Administration).

Hey—*anyone* can be an M.B.A., even if he or she is not that interested in business. Eudora Welty, the famous American author, got hers from Columbia. John F. Kennedy put in a *brief* stint at Stanford. William Proxmire, Senator from Wisconsin and inventor of the Golden Fleece award, got his at Harvard. Your next-door neighbor might even be one. To get yours, all you have to do is spend two years and a lot of money at one of the hundreds of business schools now minting M.B.A.'s—or simply read this book.

H.B.S. is the second-oldest B-school in America, and though its reputation has received stiff challenge of late from more recently established competitors, everyone in the business world knows "there's no B.S. like H.B.S." The Harvard Business School formula for success attracts the young movers and shakers from all corners of the globe. In the authors' first-year section of eighty-eight there were many foreign students: four from Japan, four from England, two from Australia, two from France, one from Malaysia, one from the Philippines, one each from Ireland, Colombia, Korea, Pakistan, and India, and two from California. Why do they come? If you asked one of them, they would probably give you the same answer Willie Sutton gave a reporter when asked why he robbed banks: "Because that's where the money is."

There are two things that make Harvard special, and this book will take you step by step through each one. First is the tried-and-true case method approach to the basic academic material. We believe, as does the faculty of H.B.S., that the study of business does not lend itself to a strictly textbook approach. Rather, the emphasis is on practical decision making, using real-life case histories as examples. Besides, would you rather sit in a hot classroom for two hours studying the theory of N-Dimensional Security Market Hyperplanes,. or read about how Ray Kroc founded McDonald's? Don't bother to unzip your calculator case—Harvard is nonquantitative, and so is this book.

We've managed to distill the two years of course material at the school into a little more than one-third of this book. Each chapter of academics contains an authentic case presentation, specially "commissioned" for this volume.

The second set of impor-

TO BUY OR NOT TO BUY

In deciding whether or not to invest in an M.B.A. or M.B.A. equivalent, it might be helpful to use the formal analytical technique taught at business schools themselves—the *decision tree.* Though Harvard is certainly a good school, it is not the only one—and it may not even be the best buy for the money.

Begin your analysis by reducing the choices down to simple yes or no decisions. We might diagram the choice between doing nothing or obtaining *some* form of M.B.A. as follows:

Remember, in the 1980s, the upper ranks of business are rapidly becoming a closed shop, with a graduate business degree as the required union card. If you fail to pay your dues by picking up the basic lingo and concepts, you will soon be surrounded by co-workers babbling business-speak in weird tongues and leapfrogging you on their way to the top.

If, on the other hand, you swallow hard and go for your degree (or do the equivalent by buying this book), we can diagram your fate as follows:

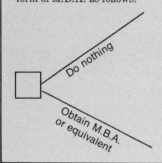

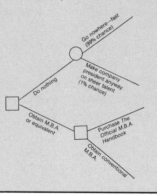

tant things that M.B.A.'s learn are the tricks of the trade that you learn *outside* class: how to choose an interviewing strategy, the specifics of "résumé expansion," the proper techniques for shaking hands, defensive and offensive phone techniques, how to handle yourself at the office Christmas party, and other essentials.

We suggest that you read the book carefully, complete all the quizzes, and practice whenever possible all the techniques we de-

Finally, to choose *where* to get your degree, it is important to get the true facts on the costs and benefits of pursuing various degree alternatives:

Rank	Institution	Minimum estimated cost of degree (tuition and books)	Estimated average starting salary of graduates	Career leverage ratio (starting salary/ costs)
1	*The Official M.B.A. Handbook*	$ 4.95	$31,000	6,263
2	University of Arizona	1,275	26,000	20.39
3	U.C.L.A.	1,800	24,600	13.67
4	University of Virginia	3,680	31,600	8.59
5	Harvard	10,500	37,200	3.54
6	Stanford	11,490	38,400	3.34
7	New York University	9,660	30,000	3.31
8	Dartmouth	10,300	33,500	3.25
9	Yale	10,700	33,600	3.14
10	University of Penn- sylvania (Wharton)	10,450	32,400	3.10
11	Columbia	10,260	31,800	3.10
12	University of Chicago	11,300	32,400	2.87

scribe. To make your experience even more realistic, we strongly urge you to simulate the classroom experience used at the school. Purchase five or more additional copies of the book for friends and associates, make up nameplates for everybody, and discuss the cases during your office lunch hours. Be as argumentative as possible. It shouldn't be long before you too are capable of solving the problems of the world in sixty minutes.

Above all, keep working at it until you can exude self-confidence when making conversation on any number of business issues, even those about which you know nothing. After all, it's often said that the mark of true M.B.A.'s is that they are often wrong, but seldom in doubt.

1

WHAT'S YOUR
BUSINESS IQ?
A Self-evaluation Quiz

BEFORE YOU BEGIN your M.B.A. equivalency training, it is important to gauge what kind of business personality you bring to your studies. There are countless self-assessment tests you can take—and some career assessment Svengalis will charge you up to $1,000 for a course on the subject. But the following test (prepared by an M.B.A. with the help of a doctor who took his residency in business) is the best and shortest such quiz we know of. Though some of the questions may appear ridiculous, bear with it. They are designed to end-run your subconscious defense mechanisms and sketch a psychological profile of your true business personality. (Answers and a grading scale are on page 14.)

Business Personality Quiz

1. Typically, you experience business as (pick the answer that most often applies):
   (a) Exhilarating—an absolute blast.
   (b) Character-building—but the best part of the day is the ride home and the double martini when you get there.
   (c) An amusing way to kill time—the people and gadgets make it all worthwhile. Where else could you make twenty-five Xerox copies of your novel for nothing, or call your college roommates on a WATS line?
   (d) A bummer—if Reagan hadn't tightened the eligibility requirements for food stamps, you'd still be on the beach in Key West.

2. You view making money as:
   (a) The root of all evil.

(b) A way to keep the wolf from your door.

(c) Simply a harmless way to keep score.

(d) A pat on the back by the invisible hand that guides our market economy.

(e) An aphrodisiac.

3. In choosing what company to work for, the factors most important to you are:

(a) The opportunity for satisfaction and growth.

(b) A high cocktail-party recognition factor.

(c) Money, cash, green, bread, bucks, and scratch . . . in that order.

(d) The best dental plan and the most liberal sick-day policy.

4. Of the following business giants, whose personality and achievements do you find most compelling?

(a) J. P. Morgan.

(b) J. D. Rockefeller.

(c) H. M. Hefner.

(d) J. R. Ewing.

J. P. Morgan

5. When you played Monopoly as a kid, your strategy was to:
  (a) Buy the railroads, collect the rent, and hold on for appreciation.
  (b) Leverage yourself to the hilt to put hotels on Boardwalk and Park Place.
  (c) Volunteer as banker in order to have "special drawing rights" on the till and buy your way out of "jail" if you got caught.
  (d) Fly into a rage when you were wiped out, screaming, "It's a filthy capitalist game anyhow!"

6. Your idea of a great time is:
  (a) A late night at the office.
  (b) Preparing a sixty-page report on the purchase-order system.
  (c) Reading *Shop Talk,* the company newsletter.
  (d) None of the above.

7. During idle moments you fantasize about:
  (a) Dropping out of the race to become a rock musician.
  (b) Getting promoted to assistant group controller.
  (c) Buying a major-league baseball franchise.
  (d) Assassinating Ralph Nader.

8. *Word association:* What is the first thing that comes to mind when you hear the word *security?*
  (a) Blanket.
  (b) Police lock.
  (c) Pacific.
  (d) 12¾ percent Delaware Water Authority debentures due 1997.

9. Which of the following tasks at work makes you feel most uncomfortable?
  (a) Laying off a loyal subordinate.
  (b) Asking for a big raise.

(c) Justifying the new Jacuzzi in Steno to the internal audit department.

(d) Shaking down your department for the United Way.

10. You don't plan to retire until:
   (a) You've made a million.
   (b) You've become fully vested.
   (c) Your position has been filled by a microprocessor or a rookie M.B.A.
   (d) You've been taken over by Gulf + Western.
   (e) The music stops.

11. Your investment philosophy is:
   (a) A penny saved is a penny earned.
   (b) It's time to prepare for the coming Ruff Times.
   (c) When E. F. Hutton talks, change the channel.
   (d) Buy silver when the fat men from Texas do.

12. What image first comes to mind when you look at the following ink blot:

   (a) The Jackson Pollocks in the chairman's outer office.
   (b) A deadly insect.
   (c) A possible new packaging idea.
   (d) Prefer not to say without first clearing it with Legal.

13. *Word association:* **What is the first thing that comes to mind when you hear the word *prison*?**
   (a) **Hard core criminals.**
   (b) **Your job.**
   (c) **I.R.S. audit**
   (d) **Limited liability.**

14. You earned your first dollar:
   (a) For getting straight A's in the third grade.
   (b) Establishing a chain-letter pyramid scheme.
   (c) Cutting grass, shoveling snow, or selling papers.
   (d) Selling grass, cutting snow, or rolling papers.

15. Your average lunch break consists of:
   (a) Mystery meat at the plant cafeteria.
   (b) A jog and a cup of yogurt.
   (c) A quick trip to the vending machines.
   (d) Three martinis and strip sirloin served by waiters better dressed than you are.
   (e) A long swig of Pepto-Bismol.

16. Overall, you feel your salary is:
   (a) Paltry, considering your worth to the company.
   (b) Stratospheric, considering your worth to the company.
   (c) Embarrassing—you're only twenty-seven, and already you make twice as much as your old man.
   (d) Hey, if money mattered to you, you would have gone into medicine.

17. Which of the following traits do you think is most critical to business success?
   (a) A good sense of humor.
   (b) A finely tuned analytical mind.
   (c) The ability to get along with people.
   (d) An inborn ability to inherit money.
   (e) An M.B.A.

QUIZ ANSWERS

Now get out your calculator and total up your score:

1. (a) 7, (b) 4, (c) 2, (d) 0
2. (a) 7, (b) 3, (c) 5, (d) 4, (e) 0
3. (a) 4, (b) 2, (c) 6, (d) 1
4. (a) 7, (b) 7, (c) 4, (d) 0
5. (a) 2, (b) 5, (c) 7, (d) 0
6. (a) 7, (b) 2, (c) 0, (d) 0
7. (a) 6, (b) 2, (c) 5, (d) 1
8. (a) 1, (b) 2, (c) 4, (d) 6
9. (a) 3, (b) 4, (c) 5, (d) 7
10. (a) 4, (b) 1, (c) 0, (d) 6, (e) 2
11. (a) 4, (b) 1, (c) 6, (d) 7
12. (a) 3, (b) 2, (c) 6, (d) 4
13. (a) 0, (b) 3, (c) 2, (d) 7
14. (a) 2, (b) 4, (c) 6, (d) 0
15. (a) 3, (b) 6, (c) 5, (d) 1, (e) 0
16. (a) 4, (b) 4, (c) 6, (d) 0
17. (a) 4, (b) 4, (c) 7, (d) 3, (e) 1

EVALUATING YOUR RESULTS

If you scored:

Between 76 and 100

Congratulations. You have a truly exceptional business personality, in the same league as Howard Hughes and Frank Perdue. You are obsessed, goal-oriented, all-consumed by work.

Between 51 and 75

Not bad. You have a good business personality but are better suited to an administrative career than to an entrepreneurial one. Don't despair: most presidents of Fortune 500 companies who took this test received a similar score.

Between 26 and 50

Hey—winning isn't everything. Your personality might be better suited to other pursuits such as arts management or house painting. Your best shot at reaching financial Valhalla is a lucky lottery ticket.

Between 0 and 25

You were born under a bad sign. Don't read any further—gift-wrap this book and give it to a friend.

2

TOOLS OF THE TRADE—

The Basic Course Material

The Buck Starts Here

FROM THE END OF World War Two until very recently, American production techniques and American products set the pace for the world. With such a decided production advantage, American business executives focused on other areas. In the 1950s the glamour field was marketing. In the 1960s it was finance. In the 1970s it was coping with government regulation.

But things have changed. While the most talented American executives were concentrating on putting together high-flying conglomerates and glossier TV advertising campaigns, the Germans and Japanese were focusing on that old warhorse, production. When it became clear in 1980 that if present trends continued, Toyota might eventually sell more cars in the United States than Chevrolet, America snapped to attention. Suddenly, the focus was on the factory, not the glass office tower. Production was *in*.

Despite the prolonged benign neglect of production, today's average executive in finance, marketing, personnel, or sales has a remarkably detailed understanding of what the modern production process is all about—an understanding best approximated by the diagram on page 20.

Filling in the Black Box

The all-purpose executive buzzword for winging conversations about production is *flow*. Flow describes how materials, labor, equipment, and en-

NONPRODUCTION EXECUTIVE'S CONCEPTION OF
THE PRODUCTION PROCESS

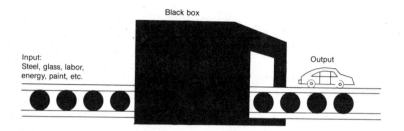

ergy move within the black box to produce any finished product from battleships to bagels. Flow can be continuous, as in an *assembly line*; intermittent, as in *batch processing*; or at a snail's pace, as in a *job shop* (custom-order operation).

1. Job shop: the preferred method of organization for one-of-a-kind products. Its key advantage is flexibility. A typical job shop is an auto-body repair studio. You name it, they can do it—pound out a fender, remount a bumper, or remove rust from the wheel wells. The job shop's key disadvantage is its high cost, as you may know if you have had your car re-

paired lately. Workers must be skilled in a broad variety of tasks, because every project they work on is a little different. Examples: a private tutor, the space shuttle, an advertising agency, a custom-built house, a one-of-a-kind Halston original.

2. Assembly line: the preferred method of organization for mass-produced items. The idea here is to standardize the product (and thereby the production process). Conveyer belts move through the factory at an inexorable pace, so that if a worker blows his nose, your new car might arrive without a left rear brake pad. But this division of labor *ad absur-*

dum does make workers very efficient at their tasks, because they perform them thousands of times a day.

Assembly lines require a heavy investment in equipment because tasks are so standardized that it is worthwhile to design special machines to perform them. Their disadvantage is inflexibility: even an insignificant change in the shape of a car's taillights requires millions of dollars for retooling. Examples of assembly-line products include automobiles, mobile homes, H & R Block tax advice, Halston sheets.

3. Batch processing: a hybrid between the job shop and the assembly line. This is the preferred method for producing a small number of similar items, such as a batch of cookies. Flow is not continuous; the idea is to group things together and send them through the factory as a unit. Examples: classroom education, tract housing, a Halston original.

There are several other terms that are important in understanding production:

• **Capacity:** the number of units per hour, day, or year that a factory process can produce, or the number of pints per hour that a factory worker can consume.

• **Bottleneck:** If cars approach a toll plaza during morning rush hour at the rate of 225 per minute, and the fourteen tollbooths can process only 75 cars per minute, you have a traffic jam. In production terminology this is known as a "critical bottleneck."

• **Balance:** a production executive's idea of catching "the perfect wave." Balance is achieved when all bottlenecks have been removed from a production process. To return to the tollbooth image, it makes little sense to spend millions of dollars on an eight-lane superhighway for commuters if they are going to get hung up every morning in front of the same damn tollbooth. It is far more sensible to achieve balance by (a) reducing the highway to two lanes, (b) expanding the toll plaza to seventy-five lanes,

(c) reducing the cycle time to five seconds (perhaps by eliminating the toll altogether), or (d) requiring carpooling.

Production in the 1980s

You have just completed the basic course in production. But don't think that the principles you have learned are applicable only to the factory environment. Increasingly, these techniques are being applied to service businesses, with striking improvements in efficiency and lower costs. Read the following case for a hands-on look at how production techniques are being successfully applied to a nontraditional mass-production business, the restaurant.

THE FEEDLOT

"It's all a matter of keeping the flow going. Basically, we've just taken the time-proven techniques of American assembly-line production out of the factory and put them into the dining room." The man speaking was Chuck T. Johnson, owner and manager of the Feedlot restaurant, the most innovative and successful eatery in Kansas City.

"When I first bought this place two years ago, it was just a smelly old stockyard, totally abandoned. This parking lot you're standing on used to be just mud, and all the dining rooms were cattle pens." He laughed. "It's not a whole lot different today, except that the cattle now pay on their way out."

Company History

The Feedlot was originally conceived in the summer of 1978 when Chuck Johnson was working as production-line manager for Ford's River Rouge plant in Dearborn, Michigan. In his twenty years at Ford, Johnson had become a specialist in many techniques of operations research: product and work-force scheduling, inventory control, and optimizing the designs of new assembly lines through the use of linear programming. His penchant for efficiency and flow was not limited to the work place, however. A busy man, he found it irksome to have his time wasted needlessly by those sectors of the economy not yet benefited by modern scientific management. This was especially true of the time he spent waiting in restaurants.

"I always got the impression that waiters weren't waiting on me—I was waiting for them," he was fond of recalling.

At sixty-four, Johnson began mulling over what business he might enter to keep active and apply his skills after retiring from Ford. He decided to combine his interest in food with his production experience. In searching for a restaurant location, he remembered an old abandoned cattle-processing operation that he had frequently driven by on trips to Kansas City. After selling his house and drawing out nearly $150,000 in pension benefits, he won a historical preservation grant from the city administration and set about renovating this century-old site.

Using the techniques of standardization and mass production learned during his automotive career, Johnson designed The Feedlot to correct many of the traditional flaws in the restaurant business. Among his innovative ideas:

• Customers arriving at The Feedlot were greeted

by the restaurant's inventory control officer, who matched parties to assemble batches of exactly forty-two diners. After being assigned a batch number, parties proceeded to the restaurant's enormous bar, "The Trough," which served as an inventory-holding area. The inventory control officer allowed each batch between eighteen and twenty-two minutes at The Trough —an amount calculated to prevent consumption of more than two drinks. (More than two drinks made customers tougher to round up.) The four-minute leeway also allowed the bar holding area to act as an inventory buffer to compensate for minor variances in downstream dining-room through-put. When the dining-room manager signaled the control officer that he was ready to process another batch, the control officer took the microphone and called out, "Batch eighty-four, head 'em up and move 'em out! Proceed to Dodge City!" (The six Feedlot dining rooms each held 210 customers and were named after famous Old West cattle towns.)

• Long, narrow tables were installed to hold a standard batch of forty-two diners each (see Exhibit 1). Because the number of aisles between tables and the elbow space per diner was reduced, The Feedlot was able to pack in an average of 1.02 diners per square yard versus the industry standard of 0.22.

• Because diners were processed in batches exactly equaling table size, The Feedlot avoided the industry's chronic problem of wasting precious seating capacity by having a party of three occupy a table for six. (A flow chart of The Feedlot process is presented as Exhibit 1.)

• Johnson limited his main-course menu to prime sirloin steaks served three ways: rare, medium, and well done. The large forty-two-person batch size allowed him to project statistically the exact mix of customer orders with a 95 percent confidence level. This allowed Feedlot chefs to begin cooking the correct mix of steaks even before diners sat down and resulted in a significant reduction in customer idle time, as well as improved customer through-put.

• The most radical innovation of all was the price: a flat $7 for salad, rolls, a beverage, and the best steak in town. The limited menu and high-volume turnover allowed Johnson to buy his steaks by the truckload, directly from the meat packer in Iowa. A computer-controlled dispenser fed raw steaks into a continuous-flow broiler, automatically cooking the meat to the desired degree—minimizing wastage and cutting kitchen labor expense to the bone.

The Current Situation

After the first two years of operations, Johnson could take great pride in the success of his new business and his contributions to restaurant science. On several occasions he had been asked to give guided tours of back-room operations by Japanese restaurateurs interested in borrowing the latest in American mass-production technology. He had also been approached by several conglomerates interested in franchising The Feedlot nationwide.

Nevertheless, with the average through-put time per customer having been reduced to thirty-eight minutes door to door, Johnson's biggest problem was to avoid unexpected bottlenecks in the system. Timing tolerances were so tight that even a brief mechanical failure in the kitchen's cooking lines could create a near stampede in The Trough. There were also occasional customers who objected to The Feedlot's techniques of insuring uninterrupted process flow. (Most complaints centered around The Feedlot waiters' habit of rubbing down tables with dilute spirits of ammonia if customers lingered beyond the thirty-eight-minute time limit.)

After considerable study, Johnson developed three possible solutions to alleviate the problem of sporadic production bottlenecks:

1. Further mechanization: Johnson was considering the introduction of a conveyer system in the dining area on which would be placed rows of rustic benches and tables. Customers entering through The Trough would no longer have to be batched. The new conveyer system would accept entering diners continuously, carry them through the eating process, and deposit them automatically at the exit. This continuous-flow system would yield an even higher throughput than the current batch processing, and the line would be machine-paced, allowing speedups or slowdowns of the line as required by the backlog in The Trough. If he adopted this innovation, Johnson was considering changing the restaurant's name to The Cattle Car. Estimated cost: $2.23 million.

2. Extra cooking capacity: Because the major source of backlog was downtime in the automatic cooking line, Johnson was considering the addition of an extra computer-controlled broiler in the kitchen. He recognized that this $185,000 machine would stand idle most of the time. But because the Feedlot's peak capacity was over 2,000 customers per hour, at an average profit of $0.93 each, he wondered how much average yearly downtime would make an extra machine worthwhile.

3. Group price incentives: Under this plan, the maitre d' would be given the responsibility of declaring a "capacity alert" whenever the crush became too great in the Trough. During such alerts, management would announce that batch price incentives were in effect. Thus, for each minute *under* thirty-eight that a batch finished eating, the entire batch would be given a five-cent rebate on the usual $7 price. Johnson felt that by enlisting peer pressure, this program could lower average cycle time to twenty-three minutes.

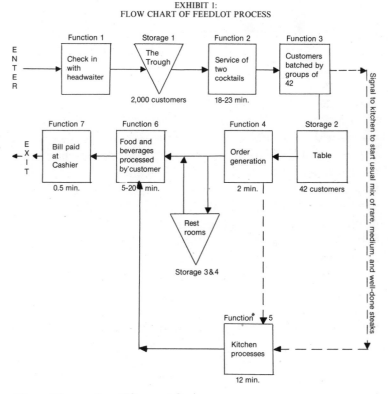

EXHIBIT 1:
FLOW CHART OF FEEDLOT PROCESS

Questions for discussion

What factors have been most critical in making The Feedlot successful: (a) low price, (b) its historic decor, or (c) its friendly, relaxed atmosphere? Which of the three solutions to the bottleneck problem in the Trough do you think Mr. Johnson should choose? Could flow in the dining room be improved by the use of electric cattle prods?

Push and Pull

"BUILD A BETTER mousetrap and the world will beat a path to your door." Or so the old story goes. These days, however, having a good product is useless without a well-financed and carefully planned marketing campaign — advertising, hype, packaging, and distribution. Diet beer, for example, has been around since the days of Twiggy (a few readers may vaguely remember the ill-fated Gablinger's beer). When Madison Avenue first trotted out this concept, it was mistakenly positioned to appeal to an overweight middle-aged audience—despite the fact that most beer drinkers are male,

under thirty-five, and acutely leery of anything that might impugn their macho image.

But then, in the mid-1970s, the Philip Morris conglomerate introduced Miller Lite with advertising that featured retired bruisers like Dick Butkus and Bubba Smith drinking Lite because it was "less filling"—in other words, more alcohol for the same amount of calories. What right-thinking beer drinker could argue with a man who ripped off the tops of beer cans with nothing but his bare hands and a smile? The rest is marketing history: diet beer is now the fastest-growing segment of the beer industry.

The essence of marketing lies in a handful of concepts known as the six *P*'s: *P*roduct, *P*rice, *P*lacement, *P*romotion, *P*roduct Life Cycle, and *P*ositioning.

1. Product is the "complete package" of goods and services you are selling. The same physical piece of equipment can be sold as several different products, depending on the customers you are aiming for. Do you sell a build-it-yourself TV roof antenna, as does Radio Shack, for $39.95? Or do you sell it only with custom installation and adjustment for $129.99, as does the local TV repair shop?

2. Price: A marketer must decide whether his or her product is (a) a "commodity" or (b) a "brand." *Commodities* are homogeneous products like wheat, milk, gasoline, or Harold Robbins novels. These can be priced only at the prevailing market rate. *Brands*, by contrast, are differentiated from each other. This can be accomplished by adding menthol to your cigarette, aiming it at women, or making it a silly millimeter longer—factors adding such undeniable value that they allow a manufacturer to charge the consumer a higher price. General Motors was the great pioneer of product differentiation: add a few hundred dollars' worth of chrome, polyester upholstery, and power win-

dows to an $8,000 Chevrolet Citation, and you get an $11,000 Oldsmobile Omega.

3. Placement: What "channels" should you use to offer and deliver your product to the consumer? "Channels" can be discount stores, department stores, mail order, or a door-to-door sales force. Different brands of the same product can be equally successful when sold through totally different channels. Maybelline is a cosmetics brand sold in every supermarket and drugstore in America. Estée Lauder maintains its image of exclusivity by selling only through top-of-the-line department stores like Bloomingdale's, Neiman Marcus, and Magnin's. Avon doesn't sell through any stores at all, but it became the most profitable big company in America by getting housewives to push mascara and bath oil door to door.

4. Promotion comes in two colors: *push* and *pull.* *Push* is what happens when you ask the guy at the hardware store what kind of paint to buy, and he recommends Red Devil over Dutch Boy. Maybe he uses Red Devil himself. But the more likely explanation is that the Red Devil marketing department is offering a six-cent-per-can price incentive to hardware stores this month so that they will *push* the product.

Pull advertising presells the customer before he or she even walks into the store; the customer is *pulled* toward a product. This presell is accomplished through massive TV and print media campaigns. Pull is what makes otherwise reasonable three-year-olds deliver nonnegotiable demands in the cereal aisles for Froot Loops or Cap'n Crunch when their mothers are trying to *push* oatmeal or Cream of Wheat.

Pull is an enormously powerful concept. Media critics contend that the advertising Svengalis on Madison Avenue can sell *any* product they want, whether it has any basic

worth or not. That's generally not true: a product must give at least *some* benefit to the consumer, psychic or tangible, to justify its price. Over a million discerning consumers obviously felt they would get more than $5.95 worth of psychic satisfaction when they plunked down that amount for a companionable "pet rock."

5. Product life cycle: Products, like all living creatures, go through a set sequence of life stages: they're born, grow up, mature, and die. In managing products, as with people, you must first determine how mature they are.

The electronic calculator is a good illustration of the four basic stages of product life cycle—introductory, growth, maturity, and decline. When introduced to the U.S. market in 1971, calculators could add, subtract, multiply, and divide —and they cost several hundred dollars. The only people who could afford them were researchers, prosperous engineers, and desperate premeds. By

1974, well into the growth phase, you could buy a simple four-function calculator for less than a tank of gas. Sales of the calculator rose to millions of units per year.

By the late 1970s the price had come down so far that the calculator was fast becoming the perfect Christmas stocking stuffer. Nearly every family in America had four or five, and the only way that manufacturers could sell them a sixth was to add sexy new features. The market was mature. But manufacturers gave it new life by introducing models capable of playing feeble lullabies by Brahms, plotting biorhythms, or serving double duty as alarm clocks.

Though the calculator has not yet reached the decline phase, its emergence meant curtains for another product that was once sold in every stationery and school-supply store in America: the slide rule. And for this a generation of math-hating schoolchildren will forever be grateful.

6. Positioning: Suppose you are marketing a dog food. There are forty-nine million pet dogs out there, and the market is too diverse for you to be all things to all dogs. There are big dogs. There are small dogs. There are young dogs, old dogs. There are meat-and-potatoes dogs, and there are gourmet dogs. If you try to please everyone, you will wind up pleasing none. Instead, you must *position* your dog food to serve a particular *market segment.*

The dog-food industry is so profitable and competitive that every year the market becomes more segmented. Once upon a time, no-frills Ken-L-Ration was number one. Then Alpo made dog owners feel inadequate if their pets didn't get "all meat." Next, upstarts began pushing bacon and kidney dinners and steak tartare snacks. Then segmentation erupted along another dimension: Mighty Dog aggressively courted miniature poodles and Chihuahuas, Hero targeted Great Danes and Doberman pinschers, and Cycle developed four complete lines of dog food, one perfect for each stage of your dog's life from cradle to grave.

This ends the basic graduate-level course in marketing. If you don't think you have completely mastered the material, go back and read the chapter again. Otherwise, turn the page for a hands-on look at how one company positioned its new product in a particularly competitive market.

"Now. What are we looking for? We are looking for the intelligent, well-educated, high-income dog owner."

MANHATTAN WATER

It was a lovely fall day in downtown Manhattan. John Black looked out of his Fifth Avenue office window and peered at the Central Park Reservoir fifty-two stories below. Then, sighing, he turned back to the group of six senior executives sitting across the table from him. He managed the appropriate smile. "There it is, gentlemen," he said as he pointed to the reservoir, "Source Manhattan." He leaned back in his chair. "We have less than six months before your advertising agency begins the official launch of Manhattan Water, and we still have not decided on a final marketing plan for the product."

Company History

The Brooklyn Seltzer Company was founded in 1906 by Nathan D. Schwartz, who invented a new process for bottling carbonated water. For many years the company dominated its segment of the large New York regional market. But in the late 1950s, national distributors such as Canada Dry and Schweppes, taking advantage of their ability to afford nationwide TV advertising campaigns and to invest in the latest and most efficient bottling technology, began underpricing Brooklyn Seltzer and driving it out of the market.

They also took advantage of an unfortunate change

in Brooklyn Seltzer's top management (see Exhibit 1). By 1980 the bottling division of the company had sales of only $7 million, versus its 1948 peak of $36 million.

In early 1980 John Black, grandson of the company's founder, was asked by his grandmother to leave his job at General Foods to take the helm of the ailing family company. Initially, he seriously considered the sale of the bottling division. But then a funny thing happened: in its September 1980 issue, *Consumer Reports* magazine ran an impartial taste test of sixty-two bottled waters and fifty-one bottled sparkling waters. Ranking first in the nonsparkling ratings, ahead of dollar-a-bottle imported waters like Pellegrino and

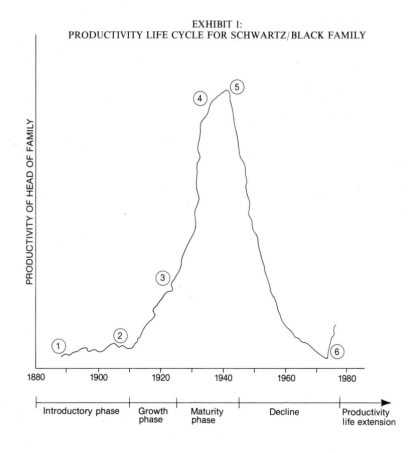

EXHIBIT 1:
PRODUCTIVITY LIFE CYCLE FOR SCHWARTZ/BLACK FAMILY

Evian, was out-of-the-tap New York City drinking water—the same water Brooklyn Seltzer used as the basic ingredient in its club soda. (Brooklyn Club Soda itself, inexplicably, was not tested.)

Suddenly, John Black sensed that the dowdy water they'd been selling all those years could be turned into a license to print money. With some advertising, a new bottle shape and color, a new name, and a little schmaltz, he was sure that the company could reposition its standard product, now dying at $0.59 a bottle, and sell it for the Perrier-rivaling price of $1.29. Black

KEY:

1. Nathan Schwartz, founder of Brooklyn Seltzer, arrives at Ellis Island with twenty-one rubles in his pocket. Saves $3,000 in twenty years working as ice peddler (1884).

2. While preparing for his morning rounds, Schwartz accidentally drops a piece of dry ice into a horse's water bucket and notices release of CO_2. Patents "revolutionary" carbonation process and founds company to market his invention (1906).

3. Saturates Brooklyn, then gets toehold in Manhattan by hawking Brooklyn Seltzer as a patent medicine during the great swine flu epidemic of 1918. Eventually dominates New York City soft-drink market and begins expansion into outlying areas (1926).

4. Nathan's son, Jacob Schwartz, finishes his accounting degree at City College and takes over operating control of company as his father

goes into semiretirement. Begins marketing product in distinctive new bottle and changes name to Brooklyn Club Soda, exceeding previous sales records every year (1945).

5. Jacob's son, Elliot Black, graduates from Columbia University in English. Spurns job working for family company and takes publishing job with Doubleday, Page & Company. Takes control of Brooklyn Seltzer upon untimely death of father (1946). Elected tc boards of New York Philharmonic (1954) and Museum of Modern Art (1962).

6. John Black, Elliot's son, is brought in by his grandmother Rose Schwartz, who still controls company. Mission: to rescue Brooklyn Seltzer from the ravages of his dilettante father. An M.B.A. from a well-known western business school and veteran of four years in product management at General Foods, Black begins revamping company operations.

picked up the phone and buzzed his secretary. "Get me Frazier over in Finance," he said. "And find out who does those great commercials for Pepsi-Cola."

The Advertising Agency's Analysis

At the request of John Black, Jerry Swiedler, senior account executive for Osborne, Eliot, Perkins, and Canzonelli, directed a three-month, $150,000 market research study to analyze the bottled-water market as it existed in 1980 and to determine the most advantageous approach for Brooklyn Seltzer to reposition its standard bottled-water product.

After reviewing Swiedler's data, the top management of Brooklyn Seltzer agreed that the best idea was to upgrade the product by moving into the fast-growth, high-profit "naturally sparkling water" category. But from his General Foods experience, Black knew better than to position his product head to head with a dominant market leader like Perrier. The alternatives were to position it as a water equal in quality to Perrier but at a lower price, or to go flat out and actually try to position the product *above* Perrier at an even more inflated price.

After weighing the choices, John Black ruled out the budget-brand approach. The new water had to be bottled in New York and shipped from there across the United States, necessitating high transportation costs that could be justified only by a high price. He rejected the suggestion of his marketing V.P. to imitate Pepsi and Coca-Cola by selling his beverage as a concentrate that could be diluted to full strength by local bottlers using their local tap waters.

The Final Positioning Decision

Having settled on the idea of positioning the water in the super-premium category and selected the name

"Manhattan," Black sat back in his chair as the advertising agency presented three storyboards (rough drafts of commercials, complete with illustrations) outlining three product positionings (see Exhibits 2, 3, and 4). The agency believed that each of these three might give the new water the image of practicality and purity necessary to justify a price $0.19 a bottle higher than Perrier's. The approaches were:

1. The snob approach, designed to appeal to upscale consumers seeking identification with the finer things in life.

2. The patriotic approach, designed to appeal to those millions of Americans who nurse a secret guilt at drinking French water when American water is of equal quality.

3. The diet approach, positioning the new water specifically as a low-calorie beverage, to appeal to a market segment that without advertising might not realize that Perrier has no calories either.

Leaning forward and cleaning his glasses, Black signaled for Swiedler, the account executive, to begin going through the three advertising approaches one more time.

Questions for discussion

Which of the advertising agency's three possible positionings of Manhattan Water will capture the largest market segment? How do you think the product will sell best in New York: in bottles or on tap?

EXHIBIT 2: MANHATTAN WATER—
the Snob Approach

1. (A panorama of the New York skyline at night. Resonant voice-over by Orson Welles:)

"Now, from the greatest city in the world, comes the greatest water in the world..."

2. (A model's hand pours the water from its bottle into a heavy crystal glass, dramatically lit. Voice-over continues:)

"...sparkling Manhattan Water!"

3. (A shot of the Central Park Reservoir at dawn. Voice-over continues:)

"Direct to you from Source Manhattan, alive with flavor and sparkle."

Client: Brooklyn Seltzer Company
Agency: Osborne, Eliot, Perkins, and Canzonelli

4. (A shot of an elegant couple emerging from their Rolls-Royce in front of the Plaza Hotel. Voice-over continues:)

"Long the water of the Rockefellers, the Vanderbilts, and now Calvin Klein ..."

5. (A close-up of the bottle. Voice-over continues:)

"... Manhattan Water, the essence of New York, is now available to you across the country, bottled with natural sparkle by the loving people of New York."

6. (Camera pans back to the bottle being held by Orson Welles as he sits down at a table at Sardi's. Voice-over continues:)

"Manhattan Water. It may cost a little more ... but at Source Manhattan, we will sell no water before its time."

EXHIBIT 3: MANHATTAN WATER—
the "Buy American" Approach

1. (A panoramic scene of a freighter docked in New York, with a crane off-loading a Mercedes. In the foreground a longshoreman carries a wooden crate. The longshoreman speaks on voice-over:)

"Working the docks of New York gives a man a mighty thirst for the good things in life."

2. (Camera zooms in on the longshoreman, who stops and speaks as he holds a crate with a large "Perrier" logo painted on the side. He narrates:)

"All day I handle the finest imports money can buy—Swiss watches, German cars, Russian furs. But there's one foreign import I just don't understand—French bottled water."

3. (He puts down the crate, produces a crowbar, opens the crate, pulls out a bottle of Perrier, opens it, takes a swig, then spits it out in disgust. He narrates:)

"Believe me, I've tried 'em all. But now America has a premium bottled water all its own—Manhattan Water! Bottled with pride by the people of America's greatest city."

Client: Brooklyn Seltzer Company
Agency: Osborne, Eliot, Perkins, and Canzonelli

4. (He sits down on the Perrier crate, pulls a lunch box into his lap, and takes out a bottle of Manhattan Water. He says:)
   "That's why my wife always packs my lunch pail with a little something special—a cool, refreshing bottle of Manhattan Water."

5. (He gets up and begins hammering the top back on the crate of Perrier. He narrates:)
   "Hey, the French can keep their water. But Manhattan Water, with the new red, white, and blue label, is America's own."
   (We close in on his face as he takes another sip of his Manhattan Water. He pauses, then says:)
   "It's too good to share."

6. (Camera pans back to a panorama of the dock. Longshoreman yells to boss:)
   "Hey, Vinnie, this crate's damaged!"

EXHIBIT 4: MANHATTAN WATER—
the Diet Water Approach

1. (Shot of Burt Reynolds on Fifth Avenue ogling an approaching blond model. Burt Reynolds voice-over:)
   "Wow, what a body!"

2. (Burt's head turns as the blond walks by him. Voice-over continues:)
   "Ever wonder why those New York models have such trim figures?"

3. (Close-up of Burt, still on Fifth Avenue. He narrates now:)
   "If you've got a second, I'll let you in on their secret..."

Client: Brooklyn Seltzer
Agency: Osborne, Eliot, Perkins, and Canzonelli

4. (Burt is now sitting down at an outdoor café, under a Cinzano umbrella. He narrates:)

"...it's the water. That's right, the delicious, no-calorie water of Manhattan."

5. (A close-up of the water bottle just after Burt puts it down on the table. Voice-over:)

"Now bottled at Source Manhattan, Manhattan Lite is the first bottled water as light as its name, with that extra sparkle of effervescence that is New York."

6. (Camera pans back to show Burt sharing the table with the same blond seen earlier. He narrates:)

"No-calorie Manhattan Lite."

(She pats his taut stomach, and he glances down. Then he looks up at the camera and says:)

"Want to know another secret?"

(He smiles, as if the cat's out of the bag, and whispers:)

"I drink it too."

Beg, Borrow, or Recapitalize

"NEITHER A BOR-rower nor a lender be." So wrote Shakespeare in *Hamlet*. This might have been sage advice for his audience living in the sixteenth century, but the Bard would clearly sing a different tune if he lived today. In the modern world of finance, the taking and giving of credit is big business, and fortunes are made and lost on O.P.M.—other people's money. Were he alive today, Shakespeare would probably be just another celebrity appearing on nationwide TV, exhorting his following "not to leave home" without their American Express cards.

Just as the average American can't live without credit, so corporations

would wither and die were it not for the availability of outside capital. Imagine you are a moonshiner from Tennessee who has suddenly decided to go legit. Instead of selling whiskey from the still within days after it's been produced, you must now age your product for at least eight years.

You purchase yeast, wood for the still, and charred-wood casks *now*, laying out cash; but you will not have a product to sell until 1990. We can construct the following time line of the cash you'd have going out and coming in at various times during this multiyear cycle.

If you could *borrow* all the money you needed during those eight years, paying $100,000 or so in interest, the deal would look like this:

Revenue	**$800,000**
Expenses	**− 400,000**
Interest	**− 100,000**
PROFIT	**$300,000**

In other words, you've made $300,000 entirely by the use of O.P.M. This is also known as using 100 percent *leverage*.

Unfortunately, life is

CASH CYCLE OF WHISKEY HOLLER DISTILLERY

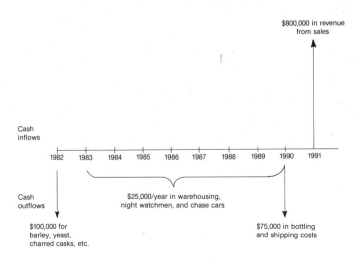

Cash inflows

1982 1983 1984 1985 1986 1987 1988 1989 1990 1991

$800,000 in revenue from sales

Cash outflows

$100,000 for barley, yeast, charred casks, etc.

$25,000/year in warehousing, night watchmen, and chase cars

$75,000 in bottling and shipping costs

THE LAST INVESTMENT GUIDE YOU'LL EVER READ

Insiders have always gotten first pick of the hot glamour investments like movie tax shelters, fine art, or research-and-development limited partnerships. And the small investor has always been priced out of the big action. But now any urban dweller can get in on the fastest-appreciating, lowest-risk investment idea of the decade: subway tokens.

New York City's tokens have tripled in value since 1970, while the Dow free-fell from over 1,000 to the mid-800s. Detroit's SEMTRA, Atlanta's MARTA, Boston's MBTA, and San Francisco's BART have also scored impressive gains. A diversified portfolio of subway-token investments has consistently outperformed the Standard and Poor's 500, and no token ever bought has been sold for less than its purchase price. Tokens also provide considerable arbitrage opportunity, especially for senior citizens, who can purchase them at a discount and sell them in the secondary market at full or near full price.

"Hard" tokens from New York's M.T.A. and Boston's M.B.T.A. resting on a "soft money" fare card from Washington's METRO.

But the time to invest is now: the federal government is moving to demonetize the token system just as it took the silver out of quarters and the dollar off the gold standard. The largest new system in the country is Washington's Metro, sponsored by Congress, which foils underground speculation by issuing paper "Farecards" instead of hard money.

rarely so kind. Bankers don't like to fight on the front lines: if something goes wrong, they want to make sure they get their money out first. As a result, most businesses are required to come up with at least 50 percent of the money in the form of equity. If our distiller finds partners to put up $200,000 and agrees to give them half the profits, the deal would look like this:

Revenue	$800,000
Expenses	− 400,000
Interest	− 50,000
GROSS PROFIT	$350,000
Less dividends paid to father-in-law	− 175,000
Profit remaining for distiller	$175,000

Still a good deal, but not nearly so attractive as before: your partners demand a greater return for their money than the bank, since they get their money out last. The trick in deciding how to finance the company is to achieve "optimum capital structure" by finding the best mix of risky debt and expensive equity. Debt may be cheap, but remember—if the public begins to prefer rum during the eight years your whiskey is in the pipeline, the bank still expects to be paid on time, whereas your father-in-law can wait.

Debt has one additional attraction: Congress, in its infinite wisdom, allows interest payments to be tax-deductible, whereas dividends paid to shareholders are not. All of us have a silent partner in every business deal whether we like it or not— Uncle Sam.

So much for the basics of finance. Now we can move on to more advanced quantitative concepts. Mastery of these topics will qualify you for an entry-level job at one of the millionaire factories on Wall Street. The math gets a little tougher here, but bear with us. In the sections that follow, keep in mind the following working definition:

***Finance:* the study of money and how it violates the rules of mathematics and common sense.**

"I'm into the takeover aspect of corporate law —
but I still play the guitar."

LESSON 1:
Mergers and
Acquisitions

Principle: 1 + 1 = 3

Nothing grabs the business headlines better than when one giant company tries to take control of another giant company against its will. The reason one firm tries to acquire another is to create a larger firm whose value is greater than that of the two component companies separately. This is known as *synergy:* 1 + 1 = 3.

What is synergy? Suppose you invented a new and improved strain of

HOW TO READ THE STOCK PAGES LIKE A PRO

Stock	Div.	P/E	Sales 100s	High	Low	Cls.	Net Chg.
StrideRte	.30	7	341	22¾	22½	22¼	− ½
Sunoco	4.50	11	986	78 −	53½	76 −	+ 1
SuprHype	.05	89	2135	92⅛	4⅞	92⅛	+ 7⅜
SynCty	3.56	8	102	31 −	21⅛	25¾	− 1⅛
SynFuel	.23		123	22½	18¾	19 −	+ ¼
SynGene		57	1068	41½	19⅜	41½	+ 10
TNA	2.30	9	344	15½	13¾	14 −	−

Issue	Div.	P/E	Vol.	Hi	Lo	Cls.	Chg.
SynGene		57	1068	41½	19⅜	41½	+ 10

Sell here   Buy here

Look for a sexy name that combines prefixes like *Syn-*, *Tele-*, *Data-*, or *Gene-* with suffixes like *-ex*, *-onics*, *-dyne*, or *-gene.* A high dividend means the firm is paying out high earnings to stockholders because it doesn't need the earnings to finance growth. These sedate stocks have *low* price earnings (P/E) ratios, which means that investors aren't willing to pay that much for them. Stocks with sexy suffixes and prefixes usually have low dividends, nonexistent earnings, and high P/E ratios.

A high volume of trading (such as 1,068,000 shares of Synergene traded on this day) for a small company usually means a stock is being touted by most brokers on Wall Street. Translation: it's overpriced.

Violent changes in price *upward* usually indicate that Wall Street thinks a merger is in the offing. Violent downward moves usually mean the chief executive has taken up residence in Costa Rica, or that IBM has just announced the introduction of a new model that will make the firm's major product obsolete.

popping corn and formed a company to sell it. You build sales up to $10 million a year, but lack the marketing expertise and money to go national. What to do? It might be easiest to sell out to a national food conglomerate with hundreds of salespeople who service every supermarket in the United States. Your $10 million in sales might easily hit $100 million because of your marriage with the national company—a perfect example of synergy. Fantasy? In fact, this story is almost exactly what happened when Orville Redenbacher's Gourmet Popping Corn sold out to Hunt-Wesson foods a few years ago.

Unfortunately, synergy is usually far more imagined than real, and in practice the notion of synergy is more effective at separating stockholders from their money than it is in creating real value. The perverse mathematics of synergy cause corporate overhead in the combined company to grow at rates far exceeding the promised growth in

revenue. Whereas each corporation once could scrape by with one corporate jet, the combined corporation requires three (1 + 1 = 3). Whereas each corporation once had a single executive vice-president, the combined corporation has three divisional presidents. And so on.

But persuade the public that true synergy *will* result from a merger, and it is willing to pay staggering premiums for that company's stock.

LESSON 2: Divestiture

Principle:
3 = 1 + 1 + 1 + 1
(a house divided into condominiums cannot fall . . . in price)

Sometimes companies become so top-heavy and cumbersome that instead of acquiring new subsidiaries they consider divesting old ones.

A firm "spins off" subsidiaries when it feels that the individual parts of the company would be worth more separately than together. This process of corporate divorce is intended to remove the need for things like the third company jet. As in any divorce proceeding supervised by lawyers, the legal fees often make the separating parties wish they had stayed together in the first place.

LESSON 3: The Efficient Capital Market Hypothesis

Principle:

$$R_e = \beta (R_m - R_f) + R_f$$

Everybody knows somebody who put $5,000 into IBM in 1947 and hasn't had to work a day since. Inspired by such tales, millions daily risk their hard-earned savings in the market, searching for the next IBM, Polaroid, or Xerox. Unfortunately, for most investors, the search for the true high-flier has been about as fruitful as the centuries-old search for the Holy Grail.

Conclusion: The next time your broker calls touting a new "hot tip," we strongly suggest that you sell the same stock *immediately*. By the time one of those "hot tips" has gotten to one of us small fry, it's probably about as hot as an Eskimo Pie.

These observations are not idle cynicism. They are backed up by rigorous research and are now dogma at all major business schools. The recently developed and statistically proved efficient market theory states simply that it is *impossible* to beat the market . . . unless you're an insider and know something that the general public does not (in which case investment in the stock is completely illegal). All non-insider information, according to the theory, instantly becomes common knowledge and is "impounded" into the stock price.

Tell your friends who made money on IBM that beating the market may work in practice, but it no longer works in theory.

Read the following case

study for an explanation of how these and other principles can bring *you* fame and fortune in the finance business.

THE SYNERGENE CORPORATION

As the case writer from a well-known business school walked in, Athos Stavropolos, president of Synergene, settled back into his plush chair. Pulling a letter off his desk, he looked up and said, "It says here that you want to analyze the merger. That's fine with me, but the real story is not in this office. Go out and speak with the investment bankers, the investors, the pension funds. Then come back and I'll wrap it up for you. Okay?"

With that, he stood up, indicating that the case writer should leave. As the case writer walked out, he wondered why he had been flown first class to corporate headquarters in California when everybody he had to talk to was back East. The thought was only idle curiosity, however, inasmuch as he was on an expense account.

Synergene

"The Merger of the Decade," as it had been touted in the financial press, had pooled the stock of two of Wall Street's hottest young firms. The first, Georges Brancusi Jeans, purchased ordinary blue jeans from a no-name competitor of Levi Strauss, stitched the name of George Brancusi in gold on the back pocket, ran ads of Jackie Onassis endorsing them, and sold them for the absurd price of $64 a pair. The second, Geneceuticals, Inc., specialized in recombinant DNA research. Though the genetic-engineering industry was at least a decade from turning a profit, it was the darling of Wall Street when Geneceuticals went public in 1980. The firm was able to sell stock for a colossal $150 a share, putting a cool $130 million into the pockets of the company's founder, an immigrant ex-stevedore named Athos Stavropolos.

Stavropolos, however, was not the sort to stop at a moderate fortune like that when he sensed <u>serious</u> money. Realizing that Wall Street would be <u>totally</u> dazzled by a combination of firms that sold jeans for three times what they were worth and sold genetic-engineering stock for one hundred times what it was worth, Stavropolos was more than receptive when his investment banker called up and outlined a possible merger.

The Investment Banker

The case writer entered the Wall Street offices of Livingston Stanley, the investment bankers who had helped Stavropolos put the deal together. As he looked at the plush carpeting, he saw a sea of cordovan wing tips. Announced by a liveried associate, he walked into the office of the managing partner.

The partner adjusted his tortoiseshell glasses and began his story. "As you know, it's a pretty depressed market out there. Stocks haven't done much since the Exchange went sour in the late sixties. It's not as easy to promote a stock price with a simple split or earnings-per-share manipulation these days.

"In any case," he continued, "the only industries that really attract attention on the Street these days are computers, genetics, and fashion houses like Jordache. About a year ago, one of our young M.B.A.'s came up with the idea of a conglomerate combining some of these industries." He shook his head with eyes closed in rapture. "I loved the idea—it was a marriage made in heaven. We put together one share of Geneceuticals at $142 with one of Brancusi Jeans at $96 and sold the package for $350. That's real synergy." He lit his pipe. "We put the issue on the market, and it sold out in minutes. It was hotter even than Apple Computers."

"But what about the future?" asked the case writer. "Is the stock of Synergene a good buy now?"

"Hard to say," said the partner. "The future just ain't what it used to be. In any case, we won't be involved again until the firms divest each other."

The case writer was obviously stunned. "You expect them to divest?" he gasped.

"Well, there's no more percentage in it for us if they don't. Besides, between you and me, how much synergy can there possibly be between a bunch of eggheads in a biology lab and the cokeheads on Seventh Avenue?"

"But if the merger doesn't stick, what was the point of it?"

The partner pointed to the painting of a young boy hanging on his wall. "That's a Rembrandt," he replied.

The Investor

The case writer's last stop was in Omaha, Nebraska, the home of Jessica Brigham, long considered by gnomes on Wall Street to be the most canny stock speculator in the nation. Brigham had purchased 10 percent of Synergene the day before the initial stock offering; the case writer wanted to know why.

"It's simple," replied Brigham. "When two fashionable firms are merged, it gives the investment community a sexy story to sell to its customers. When you add to that the excitement of a miracle drug like interferon —whose only proven physiological effect is to make brokers writhe in ecstasy—it's a gold mine. Brokers call every doctor they know and give them the story line that tremendous synergy is going to be created by the merger." She laughed. "In this case, Brancusi Jeans was going to get the genetic engineers to create clones of uniform size, with rear ends so flat that all of them —even those on the wrong side of forty—could fit perfectly into designer jeans. So, in a generation, the sales of Brancusi would skyrocket and the other denim manufacturers would be stuck with millions of pairs of odd-sized jeans." She sipped her coffee and looked incredulously at the case writer. "Pure science fiction—I love it. They must have had Ray Bradbury on retainer."

"But you bought the stock anyway."

"Sure," said Brigham. "I got in at $240 a share, since I knew Livingston Stanley was going to make the market the next day at $350. I figure this firm will go to about $700 by the end of the year before all the institutional managers dump it to reinvest in some other industry like video disks or robotics. The key is to unload first, at about $650. That's what separates me from the boys—for thirty years I've always been able to pinpoint the timing better than anyone else. It's a black art." She winked. "Of course, by now my reputation is such that it's simple. I buy a stock secretly, then leak word that I've taken a major position. It gets published in the *Journal,* and the Street figures that if Jessica Brigham is buying in, it must be good. The stock goes up; I sell off at a huge profit."

Athos Stavropolos

At last, with his preliminary research completed, the case writer made his trek back to California to the presidential offices of Athos Stavropolos. "What were your personal motivations during the merger?" the case writer asked. "Was it just money? Or did you have a personal interest in the jeans firm?"

Stavropolos looked down at his generous waistline. "Me? In designer jeans?" He laughed. "Sure, it was partly the money. And it was partly that I had a fantastic idea for the logo on the back pocket [Exhibit 1]. But mostly I really did it for humanitarian reasons."

"Humanitarian reasons?" said the case writer, his jaw dropping in disbelief.

"Look at the results," said Stavropolos. "The investment bankers and lawyers came out okay, maybe a couple million. And I got 12 percent of the outstanding shares, now worth $400 million. So everybody benefited."

"And what about the third group?" said the case writer. "What about the stockholders left holding the bag?"

Stavropolos thought for a moment. "Well—two out of three ain't bad."

"But you didn't do anything," said the case writer, almost losing his temper. "How can you and Livingston Stanley have gotten something out of nothing?"

"That's Wall Street," said Stavropolos. "But it could have happened only in America."

Questions for Discussion

Would you buy Synergene stock if on insider information you knew that its first dollar of genetic-engineering profit was not forecast until 1993? What methods do you think Wall Street analysts use to price a new stock issue like Synergene: (a) fundamental analysis of the potential profits of the company, (b) technical analysis of the market's reaction to similar issues of the past, or (c) a Ouija board?

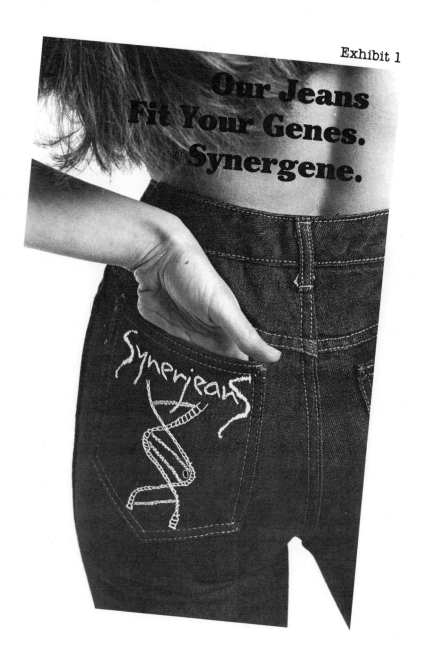

Exhibit 1

Between the Balance Sheets

NO INITIATION INTO THE mysteries of business would be complete without a brief introduction to the black art of accounting, the body of theory and convention that determines a company's all-important *bottom line*. Once you have finished school and joined a corporation, you will find that report cards now come quarterly, with the grades given in numbers instead of letters—numbers preceded by a dollar sign. But just like the grades you were given in

"In examining our books, Mr. Mathews promises to use generally accepted accounting principles, if you know what I mean."

high school, accounting numbers can be highly subjective. When your division's $6 million quarterly profit is transformed into a $3 million loss by an arbitrary change in the comptroller's method of allocating corporate overhead, you'd better be prepared to show that the loss is the fault of the accounting department and not your own.

people—are often the product of their environment. Debits that reside on the asset side of the balance sheet are good. Debits that live on the equity side of the balance sheet are bad. If you understood that, it is to your credit—which is good. If you didn't understand it, go to the head of the class anyway; the world can always use another honest accountant.

Debits = Credits

Our basic course in accounting begins with the yin and yang of the business world: debits and credits. These can be highly confusing to the layperson. Say you deposit $10,000 into your bank account; is that a debit or a credit? Simple—it's both. To you it's a debit—which is good. The bank owes you money. But it's also a credit—which is bad, because you no longer have the money in hand.

It's tough to generalize about whether debits are good or bad, however. Debits and credits—like

Assets = Liabilities + Equity

The core concept of accounting is *balance,* as is commonly illustrated through that forbidding accounting document, the *balance sheet.* To gain an understanding of how a balance sheet is created and what it means, walk through the following simple example.

Imagine you are a college student named Jacob Schiff who spots a new business opportunity. You notice that every spring, graduating seniors dump their refrigerators at fire-sale prices, and every fall, incoming freshmen eagerly buy these same "reconditioned" iceboxes at list. You decide to enter the high-rolling world of *refrigerator arbitrage*. In May you take the last $100 out of your bank account and start a company with it, issuing yourself 100 shares of stock. The company will have $100 in assets, cash, contributed by you as the company's owner.

ASSETS

Cash	$100

LIABILITIES AND EQUITY

Stock (100 shares @ $1)	$100

Realizing that you will need more capital to corner this market, you persuade your fraternity brothers to ante up another $1,000, promising a risk-adjusted interest rate of ten points over prime—30 percent. You decide, however, that this arbitrage spread is too rich to let anyone else have a piece of, so you give your benefactors a piece of paper promising to pay back the $1,000 with interest at some future date. This will be called a note payable on

the balance sheet, which now looks like this:

ASSETS

Cash	$1,100
Total assets	$1,100

LIABILITIES AND EQUITY

Note payable	$1,000
Stock (100 shares @ $1)	100
Total L & E	$1,100

Working quietly, you scavenge the halls of every dorm on campus and buy up all 52 refrigerators owned by graduating seniors at an average price of $20. These enter your balance sheet as $1,040 of inventory. Of course, you now have $1,040 less cash in your account. Your balance sheet now reads:

ASSETS

Cash	$ 60
Inventory	1,040
Total Assets	$1,100

LIABILITIES AND EQUITY

Note payable	$1,000
Stock	100
Total L & E	$1,100

Notice that both sides of the balance sheet still *balance.*

Over the summer you store the inventory in your parents' basement. In September you stake out the freshman dorms and unload 50 of the refrigerators for $50 cash each, selling the other two on credit. You now have sold the iceboxes for $2,600. Since they cost you only $1,040, you have made $1,560 profit. You have received only $2,500 in cash, however; the $100 sold on credit will be called an account receivable. Thus:

ASSETS

Cash	$2,560
Accounts receivable	100
Total assets	$2,660

LIABILITIES AND EQUITY

Note payable	$1,000
Retained earnings	1,560
Stock	100
Total L & E	$2,660

Unfortunately, it turns out that the two iceboxes sold on credit now belong to starting linemen on the freshman football team. On two successive visits to their rooms, you are given an offer you can't refuse and deem further collection efforts inappropriate. After much thought, you decide that your balance sheet should reflect the likelihood that you will never collect. Kissing your accounts receivable goodbye by "writing them down" by the $100, you reduce your earnings by a corresponding amount. The new balance sheet:

ASSETS

Cash	$2,560
Accounts receivable	—
Total assets	$2,560

LIABILITIES AND EQUITY

Note payable	$1,000
Retained earnings	1,460
Stock	100
Total L & E	$2,560

Finally, it's time to repay the loan out of your profits. You give your fraternity brothers back their $1,000 in principal and add $150 in interest for six months. After you have taken the $150 out of your retained

RATIO ANALYSIS

One handy item in the M.B.A. tool kit is *ratio analysis*. Even experts find it difficult to interpret balance sheets and income statements at a glance. Here are some quick and dirty ratios to help you translate financial statements into comprehensible form.

Ratio title	Equation	Acceptable range	Useful for
Payout ratio	Chief executive's salary/profits	No greater than 100%	Determining CEO's expendability
Acid-test ratio	(Current assets-inventory)/current liabilities	Greater than 1.0	Determining adequacy of cash level
McLuhan ratio	No. of pages of glossy filler/total pages in annual report	No more than 96%	Determining plausibility of financial statements
Leverage ratio	Debt/equity	Less than 1.0	Determining solvency
Turnover ratio	(Firings + hirings)/employees	Less than 6.7	Determining velocity of body-rolling
Profit margin	Profit/sales	Less than 98%	Determining vulnerability to anti-trust or obscenity laws
Vesco ratio	Balance in Swiss bank accounts/total assets	Less than 35%	Determining company's take-off potential (and that of key executives)
Ratio Alger	Founder's stock/total stock outstanding	Less than 50%	Determining advisability of marrying into founder's family

earnings, your final balance sheet reads:

ASSETS

Cash	$1,410
Accounts receivable	—
Total assets	$1,410

LIABILITIES AND EQUITY

Note payable	—
Retained earnings	$1,310
Stock	100
Total L & E	$1,410

A quick analysis of the final balance sheet shows what kind of year you had: $1,310 of profit on $100 of original investment. That's a "return on investment" of 1,310 percent. Not bad—maybe you should go national. In any case, if you're making *that* kind of money, you can probably forget about studying accounting. Go out and hire yourself a C.P.A.

Deciphering an Annual Report

Now that you have some exposure to how financial statements are created, take a minute to browse through that annual report that has been kicking around your coffee table for the last four months. In the old days, annual reports were printed on plain paper and were strictly business —nothing but financial statements. No longer. Today's annual report is a glossy, sixty-five-page communications link between a corporation and its fickle shareholders (E. F. Hutton reportedly spent over $400,000 on its 1980 masterpiece).

This change occurred largely during the "Go-Go Years" of the mid-1960s. That's when corporations first picked up on Marshall McLuhan's dictum "The medium is the message." They began larding their annual reports with reassuring messages from the president, color pie charts, and photojournalistic essays with pictures better than those in *Life*—even if the company's financial picture were more like warmed-over death.

The annual report is the *window* through which

you can view a company from the outside. It is of utmost importance when you're about to buy or sell a company's stock, if you're about to give it credit, or if you're considering a major corporate acquisition. But watch out for window *dressing.* Thumb quickly past photographs of smiling employees presenting checks to the Kidney Foundation; ignore letters from the president recounting how skillfully he guided the corporate ship through the twin reefs of inflation and recession this year; and turn quickly to the numbers in the back.

For the few among you who were not left five shares of AT & T by your grandmother and don't have an annual report lying around, we provide the following *annotated* one for your review, in lieu of a formal case.

This concludes the basic course in accounting. (*Note:* This portion of the book is tax-deductible if you bought it to prepare for the C.P.A. exam.)

National Student Refreshment Corporation

LEDGEWAYS
OLD FARM RD

LEMONADE
OVER 8 THOUSAND SERVED

We accept
FOOD STAMPS

Fresh Lemonad
Red Kool
Iced Coffe
LL PRIC

"Kids Making Lemonade for Kids"
Annual Report 1982

President's Message to Shareholders

It is gratifying to recount the performance of National Student Refreshment Corporation during the recession summer of 1982.

Since our last annual report our firm has undergone extensive change. As "Frankie's Lemonade" we acquired a chain of six other stands in the Greater Sudbury area and changed the name of our holding company to fit our corporate mission more closely. Our strategy of combining acquisitions with the broadening of our product line to include Kool-Aid and iced coffee has won dramatic acceptance from consumers. In a year in which sugar prices more than doubled, corporate sales rose 511 percent and profits were up to 265 percent, as the figures below reveal:

	Summer 1981	Summer 1982
Sales	$447	$2,731
Profit	$123	$ 449

That is not to say that the past summer was not without its difficulties. A suit brought by the Department of Labor was settled in August, and the company was forced to raise its pay scale to minimum wage, causing a negative profit impact of $0.16 a share. Another suit brought by the Equal Employment Opportunities Commission was settled favorably in July, however, and the company was allowed to keep its current mandatory retirement age of twelve.

Despite our uncertain economic climate, your company's management looks forward confidently to the summers ahead as periods of tremendous growth potential for National Student Refreshment and its people.

Sandy Raymond

Sandra N. Raymond
President and CEO

The company's rapidly expand

Where it all begins: The company's commodities brokers purchase forward sugar contracts at the New York Coffee, Sugar & Cocoa Exchange.

The production of fresh lemonade at one of the corporation's special clean rooms.

Key executives on the move: Symbolizing the company's continued response to the energy crisis is our increased use of transportation equipment powered by alternative energy sources.

President Raymond, representing the N.S.R.C. Foundation, presents a check to kick off the annual fund drive of Citizens to Save the Medfly.

NATIONAL STUDENT REFRESHMENT CORPORATION
Net Sales Growth

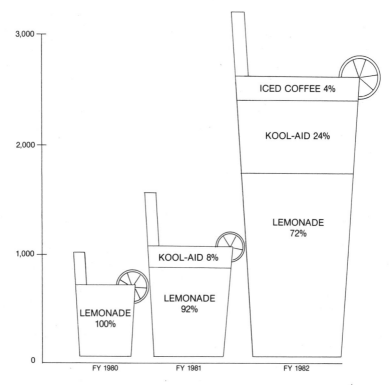

Dramatic growth in a company's earnings per share is the single statistic most often touted by brokers wanting to sell "hot new growth stocks" to their clients. If you projected National Student Refreshment's growth out 5 more years at its current rate, it would earn $526 per share. As any broker would tell you, you should currently be willing to pay $5,27 a share for this spectacular performance. Interestingly, such a price for each of the 52 shares outstanding would make this firm worth $278,256 at market value. Conclusion: its much easier to quadruple profits going from $100 to $400 than from $400 to $1,000 or $4 million to 16 million.

National Student Refreshment Corporation
Income Statement for Year Ending August 31, 1982

	1982	1981
Net sales	$2,731	$ 447

OPERATING COSTS AND EXPENSES:		
Frozen lemonade	319	55
Kool-Aid	82	11
Coffee	29	—
Sugar	326	35
Bagged ice	123	21
Stand maintenance	72	19
Labor	916	113
Depreciation	115	61
Contributions to Patrolman's Benevolent Association	225	5
Retirement plan contributions (Note 1)	36	4

OTHER INCOME (gain realized on disposition of 1963 Schwinn Roadmaster)	20	—

INTEREST	19	—

INCOME BEFORE TAXES	$ 449	$ 123
EARNINGS PER SHARE	$0.85	$0.23

National Student Refreshment Corporation
Balance Sheet for Year Ending August 31, 1982

ASSETS	1982	1981
Cash and cash equivalents (Note 2)	$ 42	$ 2
Accounts receivable (net of allowance for doubtful accounts of $10 in 1982 and $7 in 1981)	8	6
Inventory	53	23
Stand equipment (less accumulated depreciation)	26	14
Transportation vehicles (less accumulated depreciation) (Note 5)	367	208
Goodwill	10	—
TOTAL ASSETS	$506	$253

LIABILITIES AND EQUITIES		
Loans payable (Note 5)	$ 12	$172
Accounts payable	17	96
Taxes payable (Note 6)	—	—
Long-term debt (Note 5)	238	195
Common stock (shares authorized, 12,500; shares outstanding, 528)	25	25
Retained earnings	214	(235)
TOTAL LIABILITIES AND EQUITIES	$506	$253

Notes to Financial Statements

NOTE 1: EMPLOYEE RE-TIREMENT PLAN

Amounts charged to income for retirement plans were approximately $36 in 1982, and $27 in 1981. The actuarially computed value of vested benefits exceeded the fund assets by approximately $14,408 at June 31, 1981, the last valuation date available.

NOTE 2: CASH AND CASH EQUIVALENTS

The Cash and Cash Equivalents account represents $23 in U.S. currency, mostly in coin. The remaining $19 in the account includes sundry items taken in barter by our lemonade stand operations. The following barter items are included in this account and valued as follows:

3 packs of Bubble-Yum	$.60
12 Marvel comic books	3.00
Food stamps, USDA	15.40

NOTE 3: SUBSEQUENT EVENT

In September 1982 the company agreed in principle to acquire a controlling interest in the lawn-mowing and snow-shoveling operations of Jimmy Butler of 140 Spruce Street, which currently serves the same geographical market as NSRC. It is the opinion of management that this combination will result in considerable synergy for the company. The transaction is subject to the negotiation and execution of a definitive merger agreement, as well as approval by President Raymond's and Mr. Butler's parents.

Under the agreement, the company will issue one share of its common stock for each outstanding share of Mr. Butler's paper route. Additional consideration in the form of six Kiss albums and one left-handed catcher's mitt is anticipated. The value of this additional consideration is estimated at $27.

NOTE 4: INVESTMENTS

The firm's only nonoperating investment activity is in currency speculation. The company coin collection consists of quarters, dimes, nickels, and pennies and is accounted for separately from coin in the Cash and Cash Equivalents account. During the year ended August 31, 1981, $25 of currency investments were returned to the

Cash account to meet current working capital requirements. (The coin collection is valued at the lower of cost or market, $28. Independent numismatic appraisal, however, has valued the collection, which includes a 1955 double-struck Lincoln head penny, at $1,512.)

NOTE 5: LOANS PAYABLE AND LONG-TERM DEBT

Loans payable represent advances against President Raymond's weekly allowance and are secured by the inventory of the firm.

Long-term debt represents three five-year first mortgages held by Mr. and Mrs. Frank Raymond, Sr., and secured by the officers' bicycles.

At August 31, 1982, the company and its subsidiaries had unused lines of credit of approximately $157, including $34 in commitments from Junior Achievement expiring in mid-1983, and $50 from President Raymond's grandmother, expiring when she does.

Compensating balances and commitment fees are not material and there are no significant withdrawal restrictions.

NOTE 6: INCOME TAXES

No provision for either state or federal income taxes has been made, because the company is still shielded by a tax loss carry-forward stemming from four years of operations under the feckless management of the president's older brother.

NOTE 7: CONTINGENT LIABILITY

The company has been named in several pending actions, including a class-action suit filed by the Coca-Cola Bottlers of Ohio for alleged unfair marketing practices and predatory pricing. Additionally, an action is pending by the Occupational Safety and Health Administration that would require the company to provide portable on-site toilet facilities for stand locations.

Although it is not feasible to predict or determine the outcome of such actions, it is the opinion of management that they will not result in any liability that would have a material adverse effect on the company's financial position.

Auditor's Opinion

Board of Directors
National Student Refreshment Corporation
Sudbury, Massachusetts

We have examined the balance sheets of National Student Refreshment Corporation as of August 31, 1981 and 1982, and the related statements of income and retained earnings and changes in financial position for the years then ended. Our examinations were made in accordance with generally accepted auditing standards and accordingly included such tests of the accounting records and such other auditing procedures as we considered necessary.*

In our opinion, subject to ** final settlement of several pending legal actions (see Note 7), the financial statements referred to above present fairly the financial position of NSRC at August 31, 1982 and 1981, and the results of operations and changes in their financial position for the years then ended, in conformity with generally accepted accounting principles *** applied on a consistent basis.

Quakenbush & Howe

QUAKENBUSH & HOWE
Certified Public Accountants

* However, if they made too many procedures necessary, given their usual limiting rates of $154/hour, National Student Refreshment will either have to find a less conscientious firm next year or file for Chapter XI.
** The phrase "subject to" in an auditor's opinion letter is his subtle way of saying that the financial statements may not be telling it like it is. Translation: read the referenced footnotes very carefully.
*** Put any 100 accountants in a room and you'll get 101 interpretations on what "generally accepted accounting principles" are.

SEATED

* **Nancy D. Farr,** 11, Vice-President of Employee Morale and Parental Relations
* **Mikey S. Forrio,** 11, Vice-President of Finance, Comptroller
* **Sandra N. Raymond,** 12, President and CEO
* **Betsy Z. Stein,** 12, Vice-President of Regulatory and Governmental Affairs
* **Skipper B. Raymond,** 12, Vice-President of Stand Operations

STANDING

Frank M. Raymond, Jr., 15,

retired as President in 1979, Outside Director and currently Chairman of the Executive Committee

Mrs. Sally A. Raymond, 38, Outside Director and Special Vice-President of Quality Control

Mr. Francis N. Raymond, Sr., 40, Outside Director and the Company's Investment Banker

* **Elizabeth W. Barlow,** 11, Vice-President, Acquisitions and Strategic Planning

* Management directors

76

Corporate Psychiatry

THE STUDY OF HOW TO motivate people in organizations is not new. Most business people forget that the granddaddy of organizational management was Niccolò Machiavelli, author of the best-selling fifteenth-cen- tury how-to book, *The Prince.* But organizational behavior did not become a formal intellectual disci- pline until the Great Depression, when thou- sands of psychiatrists sud- denly found their couches empty. Five bucks an hour

wasn't cheap—and besides, their patients didn't have time to worry about getting in touch with their feelings when it was a daily struggle just to feed the kids.

Looking around, a few of these unemployed pioneers decided that the only depression victims still able to pay their fees weren't people at all; they were big, ailing corporations. Hence, how intellectual disciplines are formed.

O.B. is essentially enhanced common sense. But to study it formally, you must be able to speak the language of its practitioners. After all, without jargon, there would be no need for experts. Get out the dictionary and memorize as many four- and five-syllable words as possible. Then study the table below and practice translating a few common-sense ideas into the corresponding O.B.-speak:

Common-sense Idea	Corresponding O.B. Jargon
Always say please and thank you.	Always practice mutuality of respect in organizations using conversational bookends.
Employee bowling on Wednesday nights	The Voluntary Association in Corporate Life: A Search for Meaning
When in Rome, do as the Romans do.	Observe the cultural norms and rituals of your host environment.
Apple polishing.	Managing upward.
Look before you leap.	Develop a detailed action plan before commencing your implementation phase.

"You've got people skills—you fire him."

It may sound difficult to make up phrases like this, but you will get the hang of it after a while. The trick is to learn which terms are current and which passé. *"In"* words and phrases are things like *consensus, quality of work life, organizational matrix,* and *self-actualization. "Out"* terms are things like *prompt, efficient, decisive,* and *You're fired.*

Though organizational behavior is sometimes dismissed as a touchy-feely "soft science," you must take it *very* seriously. You can build your better mousetrap and raise the money to make and market it right, but without a solid grounding in how to make your organization do your bidding, you will be dead in the water. Organization can be everything.

Remember, properly organized, even crime pays.

Sources of Motivation

The first thing you must understand in studying organizations is what makes people tick. This gives you a wide variety of *action levers* to use—with varying degrees of subtlety —to make your employees hustle. State-of-the-art O.B. theory recognizes three main sources of worker motivation: (a) the need for achievement, (b) the need for power, and (c) the need for affiliation. This academic menu of motivation sources, however, is still not subscribed to by all companies. There are still a few holdouts who continue to rely on a primary motivator that has proved surprisingly durable over the centuries: the need for money.

Which "motivation levers" you pull as a manager depends, ultimately, on your *own* sources of *power*. The successful manager has five in his repertoire, beginning with the power to reward and the power to punish. Commonly referred to as the carrot and the stick, these are relatively crude techniques, according to modern organizational theory, but can be strong motivators. Examples of reward power: a promotion, a salary increase, the keys to the executive washroom.

Examples of punishment power: a demotion, a transfer to Newark, loss of access to the office football tickets.

The other three types of executive power are more genteel. "Referent" power is like hero worship, best defined as the power Mr. Spock holds over millions of "Star Trek" fans. He never existed in real life. He hasn't even been on prime time for ten years. Yet throngs still emulate his style at Trekkie conventions. "Legitimate" power is the formal authority held by a judge, a traffic cop, the Pope, or your boss —by virtue of their positions.

Finally, there is "expert" power—the respect accorded by the public to those they consider "experts" in a particular field. Expert power is commonly wielded by doctors (in medical matters), lawyers (in legal matters), consultants (in business matters), and actors like Jane Fonda (in all matters pertaining to nuclear power and corporate responsibility).

The Three Styles of Management

One of the important techniques of organizational behavior is to imagine that every organization is like a foreign country, with its own style of dress, language, and customs. These differences in style are collectively known in O.B. as an organization's "culture." But just as paleontologists divide prehistoric time into the Paleolithic and Neolithic periods, so organizational behavior specialists divide office cultures into three theoretical types: Theory X, Theory Y, and Theory Z. (Theories A through W all had their day but have been generally scrapped as unworkable. They are still observable, however, in the Italian military, the Russian farm sector, the British space program, and the U.S. Congress.)

The Theory X era began in England during the late 1700s, and the type of office (or factory) it fostered was commonly called the *sweat shop.* The assumption: given the choice between working and drinking coffee, most hirelings will drink coffee. Under Theory X, the boss was boss and the workers were grateful to have a job. Though some revisionist historians disparage this period, the sweat-shop era saw America grow from a less-developed country to the greatest industrial power in the world. *Efficiency* was the watchword.

Theory X was gradually supplanted with the invention of the affluent society after World War Two. By the 1960s, social egalitarianism was in; authority was out. The idea behind Theory Y was that, deep down, employees want to do a good job but are often stymied by arbitrary rules like having to come to work every day. *Equality* was the watchword: being liked by your employees was more important than being respected by them. The Theory Y approach is usually known as the "office without walls." It is far and away the most com-

mon office or factory culture observable today.

But as American productivity fell out of bed during the reign of Theory Y, executives looked for deliverance from the wise men of the East. By the early 1980s, the fastest-growing Japanese import was not TV sets but a novel approach to the office and factory environment— Theory Z. In a nutshell, the theory says that workers will show greater job commitment if the company shows it "really cares." The watchword is *loyalty:* in Japan employees are hired for life, and firings are unknown; if a highly paid executive screws up, he is quietly exiled to the company cafeteria at his current salary, where he spends the rest of his life serving soup in public humiliation.

Theory Z, when applied to American work environments, goes by the name of the "brave new office." Worker participation is sought by means of "quality circles," where the members of a production line or office rap with management once a week about how to do the job better.

Today, American executives are getting behind Theory Z like there's no tomorrow; in the spring of 1981 a book on it quickly became a best-seller. And organizational behavior specialists are rooting hard for its success, if only because it is the last theory in the alphabet.

Like blood types, these theories don't mix. We provide the following detailed guide to the essential differences between Theory X, Theory Y, and Theory Z (see overleaf).

Questions for Discussion

This concludes the basic course in organizational behavior. Your case assignment is to perform a *cultural audit* of your own office or company. Is it driven by Theory X, Theory Y, or Theory Z? Or does it best exemplify Newton's theory of inertia?

	THE SWEAT SHOP (1870–)	THE OFFICE WITHOUT WALLS (1970–)	THE BRAVE NEW OFFICE (1980–)
1. WORKING HOURS	(a) *Theory X*: Employees arrive at 6:45 A.M., 15 minutes before their bosses, eat lunch at their desks, and head for the door just after the boss leaves, at 7:15 P.M.	(b) *Theory Y*: Workers come and go at the office according to their circadian rhythms, an innovation known as Flextime. They don't see their bosses for weeks at a time; all communication is via pink "While You Were Out" memo pads.	(c) *Theory Z*: Employees arrive at 8:00 A.M. for group calisthenics and singing of the company anthem. Lunch is eaten during the one-hour quality conferences. Workers head home no later than 5:02 P.M. in order to be refreshed and worthy of the challenge of tomorrow's work day.
2. TREATMENT OF SECRETARIES	(a) *Theory X*: "Miss Peterson, type this letter and give me three clean carbons."	(b) *Theory Y*: "Ms. Peterson, I deliberately sidestepped gauche questions about your typing when I hired you last month. But would you consider getting this letter out for me this week?"	(c) *Theory Z*: "Agnes-san, your superior typing performance this month brings much honor on our humble sales office. Take this letter as a token of our appreciation and type it."
3. DELIVERING A LATE REPORT	(a) *Theory X*: "Sir, here is your report. My apologies for its brevity, but it was difficult to include more than fifty pages of detail since I received the assignment at ten o'clock last evening."	(b) *Theory Y*: "Fred, got some rough notes on that report you wanted last week. Sorry about the delay, but I was away on one of those three-day off-site interpersonal skills workshops."	(c) *Theory Z*: "Mitsuo-san, here's the report. So sorry it's ten minutes late, but the company was counting on my knuckleball to uphold our record against the Toyota U.S.A. All-Stars this morning."

	(a) Theory X	(b) Theory Y	(c) Theory Z
4. ASKING THE BOSS FOR A RAISE	(a) *Theory X:* "Sir, I've been with the firm ten years now and have begun to think of marriage. Do you think you might consider giving me a raise of two dollars a week?"	(b) *Theory Y:* "Fred, my wife makes 20 percent more salary than I do, and she gets free day care and unlimited COLA. Match it or I'm splitting."	(c) *Theory Z:* "Mitsuo-san, we can no longer bear to live with the dishonor of making 15 percent less than our counterparts at Avis, even though we try harder" (draws hari-kari sword). "I would be most grateful if you would act as my second."
5. THE BOSS'S OFFICE	(a) *Theory X:* A dark-paneled office dominated by a huge mahogany desk. Smoking his cigar behind it, the boss could make any visitor fidget like a schoolchild.	(b) *Theory Y:* The boss's door is always open, and his visitors are made comfortable on oatmeal-colored couches placed around a coffee table laden with back issues of *Fortune* and the *New Republic*.	(c) *Theory Z:* The boss is never in his office—he's always down on the plant floor, talking with workers or describing the new system to members of the business press.
6. INCENTIVE SYSTEMS	(a) *Theory X:* Meet your divisional profit goals, and you get to keep your job.	(b) *Theory Y:* Come within spitting distance of meeting your personal growth objectives, and you don't have to worry about a thing.	(c) *Theory Z:* Meet your divisional profit goals, and you earn undying respect and loyalty.
7. HOW EMPLOYEES ARE FIRED	(a) *Theory X:* A pink slip in Friday's pay envelope, with notice to have your desk cleaned out by lunch.	(b) *Theory Y:* The employee is taken to an expensive lunch by the boss and the personnel officer, is asked to sign a letter promising not to instigate age or sex discrimination suits, and is given six months' free use of the office phone and copier to help find another job—and himself.	(c) *Theory Z:* They aren't.

The Big Picture

CORPORATE STRATEGY is for self-styled big-picture types, and it's a lot of fun. Although originally a military concept, strategy has now been thoroughly co-opted by the business world. In the past year, in fact, the word *strategy* has finally eclipsed *bottom line* and *takeover* as the most overworked buzz-word in the executive lexicon. Face it: would you rather sit with the generals planning a billion-dollar corporate acquisition, or fight it out in the company foxholes?

What is corporate strategy? Basically, it's a way of comparing your company's strengths with the changing competitive environment in order to get an idea of how best to compete in the marketplace. To formulate a strategy, you must first ask yourself a few questions. What is your market position? Are you caught in a squeeze play between a market-dominating supplier and an equally monolithic customer? Or do you have enough market power to demand lower prices from your suppliers and higher prices from customers? A good way to demonstrate your ability to think in corporate cinerama is to knock 'em cold at meetings—any meetings—with this deadly challenge: "What business do you *think* we're in?" Or the variant, "What is our *mission?"*

Of course, the question of what business you *are* in is not always easy to answer. Take the case of an underwear manufacturer whose original corporate mission was "to provide low-cost undergarments for the people of America at a fair profit." The company later branched out into raincoats; the corporate mission became "to provide low-cost protective clothing for the people of America at a fair profit." Next it added a construction company that specialized in low-cost housing. The new corporate mission: "to provide low-cost protection from the elements for the people of America at a fair profit." Recently, the company acquired something completely unrelated, an adult-film distributor. Now the corporate mission is the all-encompassing "to make a buck anywhere we can at a fair profit."

Who can forget Henry Ford's statement in the 1950s that "tail fins are here to stay," right before his company dropped $300 million on the Edsel? Or Johnson & Johnson's folly in trying to take on Procter & Gamble's Pampers—and losing tens of millions of dollars before withdrawing from the battlefield? No corporate president in his right mind would ever want to be caught dead tak-ing the responsibility for such an unfortunate decision. Fortunately, in this day and age he doesn't have to. Instead, for $50,000 a month and up, he can call in a present-day industrial soothsayer—the "strategy consulting" firm, thereby transferring culpability—while still collecting his six-figure salary. *

What business *are* we in? Or businesses? And what should we be doing about it? The question is particularly important—and also difficult—for today's conglomerates. Consider General Electric, whose $25 *billion* in sales dwarfs the gross national product of most countries in the United Nations. GE makes everything from jet engines to toaster ovens, and its chief executive has a problem: how to keep track of how ten thousand different

* Consulting firms also provide a second service to the economy by absorbing large quantities of newly minted M.B.A.'s each year —at salaries of more than $1,000 a week. In this way they temporarily remove many of the most dangerous young decision makers from the competitive arena.

"Would a study shut them up?"

products are doing. Which ones are profitable, which are growing, which require massive investment, and which should be unloaded pronto? Without a simple framework to help make these decisions, the task would be mind-boggling.

To the rescue comes the "growth/share matrix," brought to you courtesy of a small firm called the Boston Consulting Group.

BCG's innovation was to simplify an impossibly complicated set of business activities into terms even a child could understand: "Star," "Cash Cow," "Problem Child," and "Dog." The trick in applying the growth/share matrix is to label each of your businesses as belonging to one of the four categories, as shown below:

THE GROWTH-SHARE MATRIX

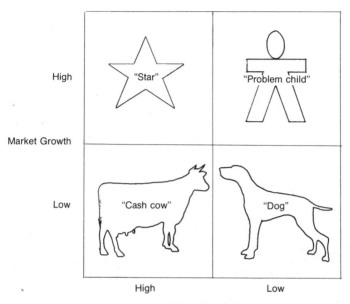

Market Growth

High · "Star" · "Problem child"

Low · "Cash cow" · "Dog"

High · Low

Market Dominance

KEY:

1. Cash Cow: a product that dominates a mature, no-growth industry, throwing off profits. The strategy here is to "milk" the product for everything it's worth, reinvesting all profits into other products with more growth potential. A good example of a Cash Cow, for General Electric, is the sixty-watt Soft White light bulb.

2. Star: a dominant product in a fast-growing market. To maintain your strong position, you have to invest major amounts of cash—to build bigger plants, keep up with major advances in technology, and so on. Naturally, the source of this investment capital is your company's Cash Cows. An example of one of GE's Stars: communications satellite technology.

3. Problem Child: a growing market in which you're no better than a small fry. The proper strategy: if you're the risk-averse, grandmotherly type, divest and breathe a sigh of relief. If you're a gunslinger, invest in the market's growth, hope you can eventually dominate, and pray. The trouble with Problem Children is that they are tremendous cash drains and may never stop asking their parents for an allowance. A good example for GE: the computer industry, growing like gangbusters, but dominated by another company—IBM.

4. Dog: a loser, the Problem Child who is thirty-three years old and never left home. The market is shrinking, and you are one of the unprofitable companies in it. The suggested strategy: identify your Dogs while they're still Problem Children and sell them off before it's too late. An example of a dog in GE's product portfolio is the nuclear reactor division, which has been a massive cash drain for years because of plant-licensing delays, contract cancellations, and *The China Syndrome.*

Why the obsession with market dominance? Is there something to it, or is it merely a macho game? Market dominance is important because the more widgets you produce—and the more experience you have in producing them—the less they cost. Imagine that Chrysler and General Motors each decided to bring a new subcompact car to market. For each manufacturer, it costs perhaps $400 million in research, design, engineering, and factory remodeling to get that first car off the production line. The second car might cost as little as $1,000. But GM has the dominant market position. If it sells three times as many cars as Chrysler, it can spread that initial $400 million three times more thinly: the same car that costs Chrysler $8,200 to produce might cost GM only $7,000. If consumers perceive that both models are identical and are willing to pay $8,000 for them, is it any wonder that GM is usually profitable and Chrysler isn't?

Ford Edsel Bermuda, 1958

In other words, if all else is equal, the largest company in an industry will have the lowest production costs and thereby command the greatest profits. But all else is not always equal. Take the pen industry, where companies compete on dimensions other than cost: quality, service, distribution, prestige, and the ability to write "first time every time" after being shot from rifles. Bic's strategy is to sell a basic pen for less money than anyone else—and to sell about a billion of them a year. Cross, on the other hand, realized that some consumers were willing to pay ten to a hundred times more than the price of a Bic for a higher-quality writing implement with more aesthetic appeal. Both strategies work; both Bic and Cross are profitable companies. The companies that aren't profitable are those caught in between: those trying to sell low-priced pens but who can't sell as many as Bic—and who therefore have higher costs of production—or those trying to produce high-priced pens but who can't sell them for as high a price as Cross.

In most industries, therefore, this relationship between number sold each year and profitability looks something like a U-shaped curve. This is the hottest concept in the world of strategy today. In fact, had you just been given this same ten-minute lecture by a projector-toting consultant, you would have just parted with a little over $30.

Use these techniques of product portfolio analysis, relative production costs, choice of competitive positioning, and profitability analysis to evaluate the strategies described in the following case presentation.

The Problem in 1976

"Eh, Michael . . . so what we gonna do?"

The man speaking was Don Vito Corleone. His hair was a distinguished shade of gray, his body hard, oversized. He was speaking to his youngest son, Michael, a recent graduate of business school.

"Papa, I just don't know. I think we need to bring that big-gun consulting firm back again." He looked at his watch: midnight. "Some of my classmates are probably working there right now."

The elder Corleone frowned. As the result of work done six years earlier, in 1969, by the Miami Consulting Group (MCG), the Corleone family operations had experienced unprecedented growth. But now the New Jersey State Legislature had just passed a bill legalizing casino gambling in Atlantic City. How would that impact the Corleone family businesses?

EXHIBIT 1:
THE CORLEONE FAMILY GROUP
Organization Chart in 1969

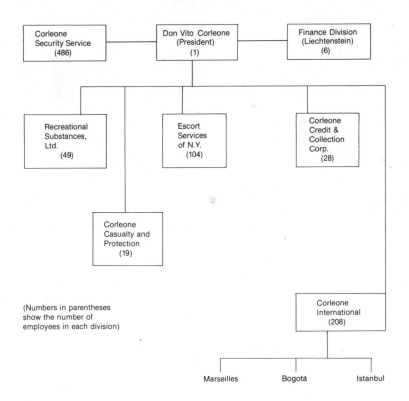

Industry Background

Businesses such as the Corleone Family Group
were organized many centuries ago, in Europe. During
the early years of the twentieth century, however,
many of these firms organized subsidiaries in large
cities across the United States. Several of them, including the Corleone family, moved their operations across
the Atlantic entirely. These companies experienced ex-
plosive growth between 1919 and 1934, during Prohibition. Key success factors included well-developed
import/export operations, well-positioned liquid cash
reserves, and strict enforcement of contracts.

Following World War Two, however, the changing
world economy brought an increasingly international
character to the industry. Most firms opened trading
bureaus in Istanbul, Marseilles, and Bogotá, as well as
other cities.

For many years the growth of the industry has
been remarkably unconstrained by the necessity of
paying taxes. Typical fixed costs include providing incentive compensation for key government officials in
host countries and employing a large number of highly
trained security guards to protect the firm and key
management from involuntary liquidation.

The 1969 Crisis

By the late 1960s the Corleone Group had become
highly diversified, with annual revenues of nearly $90
million and profits of over $48 million. Don Vito, how-
ever, had become increasingly concerned about certain
fundamental changes in some of the markets served by
the company.

Escort Services of New York, the oldest division, was experiencing a deep decline in capacity utilization because of growing free competition.

Of most concern to the Don, however, was the intense competition provided in the last year to Recreational Substances, Ltd., the family's largest division. Recreational Substances historically had enjoyed a 95 percent share of the Greater New York market. In the last year, however, the rival Sollozo Group had backward-integrated into poppy fields in Afghanistan and was about to enter the market by underpricing the Corleones by 50 percent.

The Don was wondering whether he needed to adopt the classical solution of asking the president of the rival Solozzo Group to take an early retirement. Alternatively, perhaps the Corleones should backward-integrate as well. In recent months the Don had priced land in several locations throughout Asia and had considered a hostile takeover of the Burpee Seed Corporation of Warminster, Pennsylvania.

But of even greater concern to the Don than these specific product issues was his firm's lack of management depth and long-range planning. Most members of his executive committee had experience only in narrow functional areas, such as high-efficiency debt collection, transportation and Customs management, and labor relations. The Don felt a generalist's viewpoint was sorely lacking. And Michael, his son, was still a senior at Dartmouth, too young to ask for advice.

Reluctantly, the Don picked up the phone and placed a call to Miami, Florida.

The Miami Consulting Group Study

MCG, a pioneer in the rapidly growing field of "strategy consulting," was brought in by the Don to analyze the Corleones' long-range objectives. They spent six intensive months and billed $240,000 to perform an industry analysis and formulate a growth-share product portfolio for the Corleone Group.

In summary, the analysis and recommendations of the Miami Consulting Group were:

1. Escort Services: Losses of $2.5 million in 1969 on sales of $8 million. Capacity utilization at an all-time low of 38 percent. A fundamental, irreversible change in the marketplace has taken place; the Corleones' competition is already pricing its services at nothing. Recruitment is getting harder every year.

Recommendation: Pretty-page the financial statements and sell to the expansion-minded Tattaglia family. This business is clearly a Dog.

2. Recreational Substances, Ltd.: Revenues in 1969 of $47 million with profits of $44 million (pretax and posttax). Sales in traditional opium-derived product lines are falling, though margins are still 95 percent. Our industry analysis indicates that the middle-class youth market for milder, hemp-based products will continue to flower over the next ten years. Exploitation of this market will require much reinvestment of profits for buildup of inventory, hiring of new personnel, and legal fees.

Recommendation: Use the cash throw-off from opium products to finance the tremendous growth in these youth lines. We suggest you gradually let your retail sales network decline, by attrition, and concentrate on the defensible positions of importing and wholesaling. This business is clearly a Star.

3. Corleone Credit and Collection Corp.: A small but profitable division. On average loans outstanding of over $11 million, interest collected was $4.7 million, with profits of $4.5 million. We performed multiple regression analyses and conclude that the demand for CCCC loans is inversely correlated with the health of the economy. The division's competitive po-

EXHIBIT 2:
PROFITABILITY OF FIRMS IN THE
CREDIT INDUSTRY

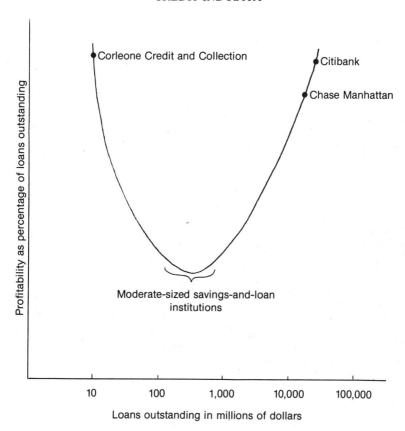

sition is strong in servicing the small-business sector, especially when the money supply gets tight and usual loan sources dry up. We recommend keeping this division small and nimble, as profitability in the banking industry clearly shows a U-shaped curve.

Overall Recommendations: Milk this Cash Cow during boom years; reinvest and expand when the economy experiences a downturn. Continue current aggressive methods of receivables management, as rapid foreclosure of overdue loans by this division has often led in the past to the acquisition of new businesses by the Corleone Family Group.

4. Corleone Casualty and Protection: A real Problem Child, this division was acquired last year from the estate of its late president, Sal Teneglia. It has only a 3 percent market share and totally lacks credibility among its potential customers, because the market is dominated by the Barzini Group, which holds the remaining 97 percent. Conclusion: The Barzinis are likely to resist any further erosion of their market share by use of their usual unfair competitive practices.

Recommendation: Divest this division to the highest bidder—which will most likely be the Barzini Family. Tomorrow would be soon enough.

The Situation in 1976

Looking back, the Don realized that MCG's 1969 recommendations had been of enormous value. In the six years since the study, Corleone revenues had grown to nearly $267 million. He had sold Casualty and Protection and Escort Services and focused his resources on his increasingly successful import/export operations. Profits were at an all-time high, and Michael Corleone had taken over as executive vice-president. But now the New Jersey State Legislature had just announced that within two years it would allow the opening of legal gambling casinos in Atlantic City.

Other regional firms from Nevada, Chicago, and Providence were sending representatives to Atlantic City to assemble prime Boardwalk real estate. The Don wondered whether he should continue focusing on his current activities or risk entering what was shaping up as an all-out competitive war for market share in the East Coast legalized gambling industry.

As he picked up the phone to request the aid of MCG in evaluating his current strategic alternatives, the Don hesitated for a moment, remembering the six-figure fee their last study had cost him. As he waited for the MCG receptionist to answer, the thought crossed his mind that maybe now was the time to diversify into the most profitable racket of all: strategy consulting.

THE CORLEONE FAMILY GROUP
Division Revenues in 1969
(in millions of dollars)

Division	Sales	Profit
Escort Services of New York	$ 7.9	$(2.5)
Recreational Substances, Ltd.	47.0	44.2
Corleone Credit and Collection Corp.	4.7	4.5
Corleone Casualty and Protection	16.2	(2.3)
Corleone International	14.3	4.3
TOTAL	$90.1	$48.2

Questions for Discussion

What is the current overall strategy of the Corleone Family Group? Why is it so profitable? Should the Don gamble on entering the Atlantic City market? Summarize the types of competitive weapons that give a company a defensible position in this industry.

3

PACKAGING YOURSELF

Choosing a Career

or

"Shall I make five million or achieve karma?"

NOW THAT YOU HAVE completed your basic course work, it is time to start thinking about which area of business you are most interested in. This is important because of the many significant differences between career paths; some are dead ends,

"Oh, if I hadn't got into stocks, I suppose I might have got into something completely different. Bonds, maybe, warrants, options, futures . . . who knows?"

while others are four-lane highways to success.

Most areas of business have at least *some* tangible output. *Production* is concerned with producing an appliance or car efficiently. *Sales* and *marketing* get the product to the customer. On the other hand, *personnel* or *research and development* departments have an output that is less tangible. Finally we come to *finance,* which deals with money and numbers and has almost no concrete output whatsoever.

If you are like most M.B.A.'s, you will tend to choose your career on the right-hand side of what is known in the trade as the "line of direct labor."

M.B.A.'s, having a rather oversized opinion of their own worth, are very sensitive about being underpaid. In addition, they know that pay levels are often keyed to one's level of tangible output, *if output is actually measurable.* Thus, managers who work in jobs with tangible output get paid appropriate salaries, while managers whose output cannot be measured can earn absolutely stratospheric ones. An exceptionally well-paid factory manager, responsible for the production of 300,000 cars a year, might get paid $100,000, max. A successful financier who works the phones all day as a marriage broker for conglomerates, and produces nothing tangible at all, can earn millions.

LINE OF DIRECT LABOR

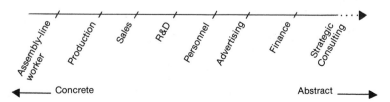

Résumé Expansion

or

"I'm twenty-three, can type, and was president of GM for two summers during college"

NOW THAT YOU HAVE DE-cided what sort of job you want to get, the next step is to prepare your résumé. A résumé is your communications link with the Real World. If you blow it here, you might as well pack up and go home. A *good* résumé will transform the insipid into the inspired, the mundane into the magnificent, the illegal into the entrepreneurial. A straight-shooting résumé will not. If you want to tell the unvarnished truth, that is your prerogative. So is unemployment.

This is not to imply that you should lie—only that you repackage your achievements in terms that give them dignity and importance, a process known as *résumé expansion*. The most important thing here is patience: if you stop writing when your résumé looks merely acceptable, any tollbooth operator will beat you out for the job. Instead, even when applying for an entry-level position, keep polishing until you appear qualified to be CEO of RCA.

With this commitment to excellence in mind, the writing itself is simple. Begin with a blank pad of paper and list the details of everything that you have ever done since high school, no matter how in-

FIFTY SUGGESTED
ACTION WORDS
(a partial list)

Abdicated	Managed
Achieved	Maneuvered
Acquired	Monitored
Audited	Netted
Awarded	Packaged
Balanced	Procrastinated
Collaborated	Produced
Colluded	Profited
Consulted	Promoted
Deducted	Quadrupled
Designed	Railroaded
Destabilized	Repositioned
Disposed	Revitalized
Divested	Selected
Doubled	Served
Established	Sheltered
Formulated	Sidestepped
Founded	Specified
Hired	Stonewalled
Improved	Terminated
Inflated	Totaled
Initiated	Tripled
Instituted	Xeroxed
Introduced	Yielded
Leveraged	Zigzagged

significant. Do not be concerned that your list is dull. It ought to be—business itself is dull. Do not be concerned that your list seems trivial. Sometimes the most trivial accomplishments can be expanded the best.

As you read over your initial list, avoid despondency. Remember that without résumé expansion no one would ever get a job. But here's where the creative fun begins. Translate the list, item by item, using the above collection of *action* words. The end product should be a résumé Lee Iacocca would envy. If not . . . translate again.

Prentiss Robert Jackson was a business student who used this technique. Born of humble stock in Scarsdale, New York, he had an academically successful but otherwise nondescript four years at a well-known midwestern college. On the face of it, he was afraid that his lack

Education:
High School: Scarsdale High, Scarsdale New York
College: North Western U., September 1977-
    June 1981
    . Made Dean's List
    . So did 82% of the class
    . Babysat a couple of times for my
      Philosophy prof. when he and spouse
      went to Chicago
    . Dealt a little marijuana to friends to
      work my way through school after
      the Old man cut me off.

Graduate Work: Harvard Business School, September 1981- M.B.A. expected in June
    1983. (God willing!)
    . Grind in library six days a week
    . Organized Saturday night parties
      to meet local college women with
      chicks appeal.

Work Experience:
Cook: Kentucky Fried Chicken, Summer
    1981
    . Biggest one in Westchester
    . Cooked on swing shift

- Took home extra chicken if I cooked too much
- Taught highschool kids how to cook chicken, and told them to hustle

Caddy: Greenview Country Club, Summer 1980
- Found golfer's balls
- Replaced divots
- Told members off when they undertipped
- Tended the pin
- Arranged member's betting pools
- Stepped on opponent's balls in the rough

Other Experience:
- Won $50,000 in McDonald's "Build a Big Mac" contest summer 1981
- Spent $18,000 of winnings on new Corvette
- Totalled car into front window of local Teamster's Union hall while coming home blotto from party
- Sold car to pay repair bills and settle with Teamsters
- Used remaining $21,000 to pay for business school.

of serious work experience would doom him to a decade of penal servitude in somebody's personnel department. Instead, by careful application of résumé expansion, P. R. was able to turn his meager summer experience into a corporate recruiter's dream. Follow along as we trace the evolution of Jackson's résumé from scribbled work sheet to finished product.

Résumé Expansion **109**

Career Objective: a position offering
challenge, personal growth,
and serious *dinero*

Résumé of
PRENTISS ROBERT JACKSON

Home address: **School address:**
12 Spruce Lane   **27 Gallatin Hall**
Scarsdale, N.Y.   **The Business School**
                                                         Boston, Mass.

Education
1981–1983   **HARVARD GRADUATE SCHOOL OF BUSINESS
               ADMINISTRATION**
               Worked my way through school by winning $50,000 special
               construction contract from national restaurant chain. (Was forced
               to dispose of major asset, however, after run-in with local
               Teamsters organization.) Founding member, Aflu-American
               Association.

1977–1981   **NORTHWESTERN UNIVERSITY**
               B.A. received June 1981. Dean's List. Established primary day-
               care service for faculty children. Paid for tuition and expenses last
               three years by founding a small business that marketed a
               complete line of leisure products to students, achieving return on
               investment of 2,048 percent. Summa cum laude thesis: *David
               Bowie: The Last Existential Man.*

**Work
Experience**
Summer   **GOLF COORDINATOR, GREENVIEW COUNTRY CLUB**
1982   Responsible for revitalization of golf course to achieve improved
               playing characteristics. Tripled player through-put by utilizing
               batch processing. Provided professional assistance and financial
               consulting services to members. Helped ensure members'
               strategic success by repositioning them vis à vis their
               competitors.

Summer   **SPECIAL ASSISTANT TO FRANCHISOR, KENTUCKY FRIED
1981   CHICKEN, HARRISON, NEW YORK**
               Senior production officer during high-volume evening shift.
               Audited inventory stocking levels and instituted control systems to
               prevent exceeding storage capacity. Conducted initial employee
               orientation and instituted employee motivational seminars.

Look, I've got a great deal in alfalfa hydroponics all put together, but I need twenty million in seed capital to get it off the ground . . .

Sounds like a tax shelter to me. We can knock off the usual limited partnership in a couple of weeks. And with the classmate's discount, the fee shouldn't run much more than half a million . . .

Did you say twenty million, U.S.? Will you accept a check!

And between squash championships, I've been given total control over the campaign for Lever Brothers' hottest new product— peppermint rug deodorant . . .

That must be fascinating. Let me tell you about my last audit on . . .

Gee, Laura, you look like the world's treating you well. I haven't seen you since my divorce. Or was it three years ago, when I took over the Southwest sales territory!

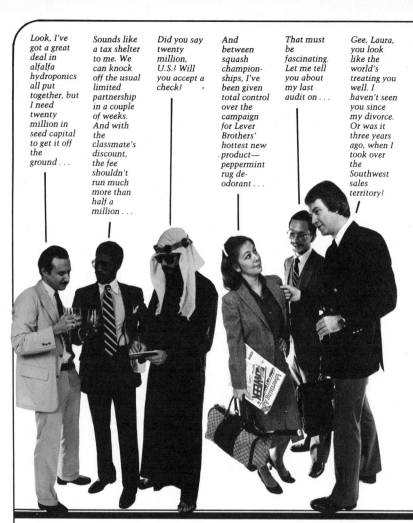

The Entrepreneur: Talks a good game, but is actually scrounging for his next meal. Wears $600 Hickey-Freeman suit purchased four years ago before most recent deal fell through. MOTTO: "Big, Very Big."

The Investment Banker: Works ungodly hours, owns beach house in the Hamptons which he's never seen. Smokes genuine Havana cigars. MOTTO: "Dress British, Think Yiddish."

The Oil Prince: Eton and Oxford grad. Intimate of Armmand Hammer, David Rockefeller, and Princess Caroline. MOTTO: "Yamani or Your Life."

The Advertising Account Executive: Spent two years at Benton & Bowles helping package "The Edge of Night," before moving over to product management at Ogilvy & Mather. Regular at J. G. Melon's. MOTTO: "There's No Promotion Like Self-Promotion."

The Accountant: Passionless eyes; graduated with honors in Accounting from Ohio State. Subscribes to *U.S. News and World Report*. Four more years of slogging before he's up for partnership at Price, Waterhouse. MOTTO: "Better Safe Than Sorry."

The Sales Manager: Ex-running back for Boston College. Drinks whatever his customers drink, only more. MOTTO: "Go for the Close."

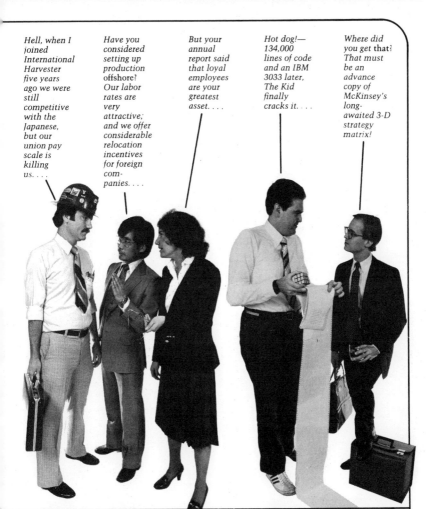

Hell, when I joined International Harvester five years ago we were still competitive with the Japanese, but our union pay scale is killing us. . . .

Have you considered setting up production offshore? Our labor rates are very attractive; and we offer considerable relocation incentives for foreign companies. . . .

But your annual report said that loyal employees are your greatest asset. . . .

Hot dog!— 134,000 lines of code and an IBM 3033 later, The Kid finally cracks it. . . .

Where did you get that? That must be an advance copy of McKinsey's long-awaited 3-D strategy matrix!

The Production Engineer: Sports company tie; wears hard hat as protection from the paper pushers above him. MOTTO: "Get It Out the Door."

The Korean Minister of Trade: American wife, met while studying for Economics degree at M.I.T. Spends eight months of the year touring Western plants to stay "current" on the latest technology. MOTTO: "Export or Die."

The Personnel Manager: Hampshire College graduate. Earned Ph.D. in Comparative Literature before switching to something employable. MOTTO: "People, Not Profits."

The Data Processing Manager: Drives an oil-burning VW bug. Makes money on the sly, running computer dating service on company's CPU. MOTTO: "Garbage In, Garbage Out."

The Strategy Consultant: Peripatetic, always suffering from jet lag. Carries battered suitcase and overhead projector. MOTTO: "Have Calculator, Will Travel."

**Fifth Year Reunion
A Guide to Corporate
Personalities**

Re-aiming the Loaded Question

AFTER YOUR EXPANDED résumé has catapulted you across the front lines of a company, brace yourself for eyeball-to-eyeball confrontation in that deadliest of all business rituals, the job interview.

On rare occasions, job interviews can actually be fun—especially if a top-level headhunter is trying desperately to lure you away from a pleasant enough $80,000-a-year job. But for the rest of us—and

"Sir, I would like the opportunity to bring the same search for excellence taught me on the playing field and in the classroom to churning portfolios here at Evans & Edwards."

certainly for graduating business students and college seniors—nothing makes your ticker beat quite so quickly as an impending run-in with a recruiter.

Sending out your résumé, after all, is like firing endless long-range salvos into the night: if some distant executive doesn't believe your claims of earning a quarter of a million dollars from a campus pizza-delivery business, he can simply pitch your résumé into the trash basket. That's a lot easier to take than watching a recruiter in a three-piece suit laugh in your face at point-blank range.

But the clammy palms and elevated blood pressure we all face *can* be minimized—and your chances of getting hired maximized—if you develop a custom-tailored interviewing strategy appropriate for each interview.

Strategy Formulation

Imagine yourself the harried corporate recruiter who comes to campus to hire three students. Plucked from your comfortable high-rise office, you are pent up for a week of eight-hour days with a parade of the most painfully eager faces you've ever seen. Eighty similar résumés expanded beyond recognition, eighty similar life stories. How can you possibly choose?

Veteran interviewers know the answer: you screen the résumés on the plane from Chicago and make your three selections in advance. If these do not come across in person as total zippos, they're in. The only chance for the other seventy-seven is if the first string strikes out.

This is where strategy comes in. The night before you face a job interview, you must think about the fit between your qualifications and the job in question and put yourself into one of the following categories:

1. I should get this job.
2. I might get this job, with luck.
3. It would be a travesty if I got this job.

Corresponding to each category is a distinct interviewing strategy. We will illustrate each approach by assuming for the moment that three differently qualified candidates are applying for the same corporate finance job with a Fortune 500 company.

Category 1: "I should get this job"

Candidate 1 has the ideal background: an Ivy League graduate with two years' experience working at Merrill Lynch before business school. He has recently published an article in *Institutional Investor* critiquing modern portfolio theory and received honors in his first year at business school.

Proper Strategy: The *confident* approach. He expects to be chosen and can afford to let the interviewer draw out the relevant facts, since they are printed on his résumé anyway. He appears enthusiastic but understated. His clothing is elegant and utterly conservative. If he doesn't lose consciousness in the interview, it's in the bag.

Category 2: "I might get this job, with luck"

Candidate 2 has a very strong record, but one that is not *quite* right for this job. He received highest academic honors in college, but in sociology rather than economics. He has two years of solid work experience soliciting corporate donors for the Crohn's Disease Foundation and got first-year honors in business school.

Proper Strategy: The *hard-charging* approach. The candidate continually tries to steer the conversation around to each of his achievements and appears overly enthusiastic. Since the interviewer is probably a man of the old school, the candidate is laboring under something of a handicap. But if he doesn't come off as too aggressive, he has a chance of getting the job.

Category 3: "It would be a travesty if I got this job"

Candidate 3 is as well qualified for the job as the other candidates from a professional standpoint, but has virtually no chance of getting it because of her unacceptably eclectic background. She graduated ten years ago from Berkeley, became an FM radio programmer for WIGY in Bath, Maine, then underwent deprogramming to become a disciple of the Reverend Moon. She ascended quickly in the organization to become portfolio manager for the Reverend's real estate empire, but fell out with her mentor over tenant removal policies and enrolled at business school. She neglected her studies somewhat to manage her personal investments and finished the first year on probation.

Proper Strategy: The *high-rolling* approach. She has nothing to lose and can't possibly get the job unless she takes big chances by refusing to give pat answers and lucks into an interviewer who finds her candor and originality refreshing.

Warning: The high-rolling approach almost never works if the job requires more than one interview.

Preparing Your Mind: A Preflight Checkout

You've spent years building your résumé and interpersonal skills for this moment. You have to be crisp, sharp, aware. But you can't let the recruiter know just how excited you are: the most prized quality in business is self-confidence and control. If you seem gushing, or nervous, you might as well kiss the job good-bye altogether.

To relax, imagine that you are not entering an interview cubicle at all, but are boarding an airplane to give the interviewer a brief aerial tour of your past. With that in mind, we'll follow our three candidates through their upcoming corporate finance interviews.

General Electric Interview 37, Room 15E, 4:30 P.M.

Phase One: Boarding

The **confident** candidate arrives precisely one minute before the scheduled beginning. He dresses in a gray three-piece wool suit —with lapels that are, by instinct, the exact same width as the interviewer's —and red club tie. When motioned in by the recruiter, he gives a firm handshake and says, "Good afternoon, sir, I am ..."

The **hard-charging** candidate arrives thirty minutes before his starting time and paces outside the interviewing booth. He wears a gray wool suit, but with lapels that are inadvertently too fashionable. He proceeds to the lavatory three times during his wait to reassure himself that no lint balls have appeared on his jacket. He has neglected to purchase black wing tips and wears saddle shoes instead. As soon as the interview-room door opens, he lunges forward, wrenches the interviewer's hand in a crushing handshake, and declares, "Oh, hello, I'm ..."

Boarding: greeting the interviewer.

The **high-rolling** candidate wears a pair of faded jeans, a turtleneck sweater, and jogging shoes—not trying to put on the gloss for anybody. As the interviewer opens the door, she folds her copy of *Rolling Stone,* shakes his hand, sits down in a chair with her feet up, and says, "I'm Jane Nugent, remember—the ex-Moonie?"

Phase Two: Taxiing

There is a pregnant silence as the interviewer and candidate take their seats. Finally, the interviewer asks his first ques-

Taxiing: a pregnant silence.

tion: "So, how do you like it here at school?"

Confident: "It's pretty hard, but basically great. I've never had a chance to work with as talented a group of people as the faculty and students here."

Hard Charger: "It's super. Of course, I miss the challenge of being captain of the national champion bowling team, as I was for two semesters in college."

High Roller: "It stinks. But I had to get my ticket punched."

Phase Three: Taking Off

The interviewer pursues his first serious line of questioning, looking for depth and a well-reasoned response: "So, what talents do you feel you would bring to our department at General Electric?"

Confident: "To be honest, I feel my strongest assets are my ability to learn quickly and my ability to get along well with people. In addition, I have some solid experience on Wall Street and have published a

Taking off: responding to the first serious question.

paper on finance—it's on my résumé, but I'd be glad to amplify if you'd like."

Hard Charger: "I'm hungry and aggressive and have always excelled in everything I've put my mind to. I graduated Phi Beta Kappa from college. I was third in my class here at business school [produces notarized transcript]. Frankly, I think that within two years of getting my feet wet I could be the number-one producer in your department."

High Roller: "I've got balls. [She laughs.] I put my boss's money into Manhattan real estate when the

city was on the verge of bankruptcy in '74. [Sits back and lights a cigarette.] Let's face it, most of the kids from business school have never managed an asset more valuable than their BMW's."

Phase Four: Cruising at Altitude

The recruiter now asks a loaded question that allows the candidate to reveal something of his or

Cruising at altitude: the applicant starts smoking with both guns in response to a loaded question.

her political views. "So, what do you think about the effect taxes have on incentives in the American economy, and is it fair for Congress to cut taxes on corporations?"

Confident: "If I knew the answer to that, I'd win the Nobel Prize." They both laugh.

Hard Charger: "During my senior year I beat the pants off the Michigan debating team with a speech on just that subject. The answer, unequivocally, is yes."

High Roller: "Who needs Congress? [Laughs.] During my years managing money for a tax-exempt organization, I learned a lot about the Law and the Profits."

Circling: the candidate, running out of time, goes for the jugular.

Phase Five: Circling

The interviewer checks his watch: three minutes to go. He tries to change to a neutral subject. "Well, we're almost out of time. Anything you'd like to talk about before we finish?"

Confident: "Perhaps I'm out of line by mentioning this, but if you do make me an offer, I presume it's okay to defer starting until Labor Day?"

Hard Charger: "Do you have much foreign currency translation at GE Corporation? I haven't had a chance to mention it before, but I'm fluent in Arabic and German, and I'd be glad to brush up on Japanese."

High Roller: "Yes, I was wondering if you have ever considered becoming an Amway distributor? You know, I made over $20,000 last year with the distributorship I built up here at business school. [Produces a brochure.] I'd be glad to sponsor you."

Phase Six: Landing

The interviewer stands up and puts out his hand. "Well, I've enjoyed chatting with you."

Crash landing.

The three-point landing.

Confident: "Thanks, I've enjoyed it, too. See you in September." He smiles.

Hard Charger: "Thank you. By the way, I've got several other highly competitive offers I'm keeping

Ditching (not recommended).

on the back burner until you give me an answer."

High Roller: "Well, what do you say, do I get the job?" If the answer is negative, or if the recruiter wants a second interview at the home office, the candidate shakes the recruiter's hand and gives him a jolt of her joy buzzer.

How to Decide on Your Approach

Deciding on whether to be confident, hard charging, or high rolling requires a careful evalua-tion of the fit between the requirements of the job and your résumé. If this proves too difficult, a common solution is to send your letter and résumé to the company and analyze the polite form letter you get in response. A careful reading between the lines here will help you determine how enthusiastic the company really is about you. We include three sets of these letters as an illustration, in pairs: one as the company wrote it, and the other offering a translation of what was really meant. For this example, we return to Prentiss Robert Jackson, the gentleman who successfully expanded his résumé in the previous chapter.

Example 1:   an encouraging letter suggesting adoption of the hard-charging approach

WHAT THE COMPANY REPLIED:

VAIN & COMPANY

STRATEGY CONSULTANTS
ONE ATLANTIC AVENUE ● BOSTON ● MASSACHUSETTS ● 02110

April 1, 1982

Mr. Prentiss Robert Jackson
27 Cornfeld Hall
The Business School
Boston, Massachusetts 02163

Dear Mr. Jackson:

    Thank you for your recent inquiry about working for Vain & Company. The Recruiting Committee has reviewed your application, and we are impressed with your qualifications.

    We hope you will make arrangements to talk with us during our scheduled days on campus, April 17-31. Since our interviews are by invitation only, please take this letter to the Placement Office as evidence of our interest in speaking with you.

    We are appreciative of your interest in Vain & Company, and look forward to talking with you later this month.

                         Sincerely,

                         H. R. de Villachaise
                         Henri Robert de Villachaise
                         Principal

WHAT THE COMPANY REALLY MEANT:

VAIN & COMPANY

STRATEGY CONSULTANTS
ONE ATLANTIC AVENUE ● BOSTON ● MASSACHUSETTS ● 02110

April 1, 1982

Mr. Prentiss Robert Jackson
27 Cornfeld Hall
The Business School
Boston, Massachusetts 02163

Dear Mr. Jackson:

Thanks for the letter and resume. We must admit we were impressed. Your ability to sling words like "strategic success" and "implementation", together with an M.B.A. from one of the less quantitative schools are the perfect qualifications for work in the glamor world of strategy consulting. And, to be perfectly honest, your previous experience isn't worth jack anywhere else.

At Vain & Company, we've experienced growth of over 30% a year for the last decade. Our own strategy is based on skimming off the best talent business schools have to offer before our large corporate clients get it. For this reason, we look on recruiting as a pre-emptive strike. We groom the finest M.B.A.'s money can buy, repackage them, and bill them out to our customers at ten times the hourly rate they'd pay their own.

We would like to talk with you to see whether you possess the appearance and style it takes to convince a 60 year old chief executive he needs your advice to run his company.

Sincerely,

H. R. de Villachaise

Henri Robert de Villachaise
Principal

BOSTON   LONDON   PARIS   TOKYO   TEHRAN   ABU DHABI   SUN VALLEY

Example 2: an unencouraging letter suggesting adoption
of the high-rolling approach

WHAT THE COMPANY REPLIED:

BLACK ANGUS PETROLEUM CORPORATION
ONE ENERGY CENTER
DALLAS, TEXAS 75201

April 1, 1982

Mr. Prentiss Robert Jackson
27 Cornfeld Hall
The Business School
Boston, Massachusetts 02163

Dear Mr. Jackson:

    Thank you for forwarding to me your letter regarding a
position with us.

    We are a small firm in the wildcatting business, and
only hire M.B.A.'s if they are exceptionally well-qualified.
However, if you're passing through Texas and would like to
stop by for an interview, please give Betty Lou a call at
(719) 143-4657.

Sincerely,

R. J. Scales

Robert James Scales
President

"KING OF THE WILDCATTERS"

WHAT THE COMPANY REALLY MEANT:

BLACK ANGUS PETROLEUM CORPORATION
ONE ENERGY CENTER
DALLAS, TEXAS 75201

April 1, 1982

Mr. Prentiss Robert Jackson
27 Cornfeld Hall
The Business School
Boston, Massachusetts 02163

Dear Mr. Jackson:

Since they wrote me up in the <u>Wall Street Journal</u> last
month as the "King of the Wildcatters," I've been getting
hundreds of letters from you overschooled peckerwoods up
North. Most of the M.B.A.'s I've met seem like ten dollar
horses with fifty dollar saddles.

The oil business is a crap shoot. When I started this
company, we came up with nineteen dry holes and kept
drilling 'til the twentieth one hit. I've never met anyone
who wore a tie who had the backbone to make it in this here
industry.

But if you want to fly yourself down to the ranch and
punch a few beers with me, all right. At the very worst,
we'll be sure and give you a taste of some three-alarm Texas
chili.

Stand tall,

Buzz Scates
President and Owner

"KING OF THE WILDCATTERS"

Example 3: the blatant rejection letter (AKA "The Bullet")

WHAT THE COMPANY REPLIED:

CROESUS PARTNERS
VULTURE CAPITAL
SUITE 900
EMBARCADERO AT THE FAULT LINE
SAN FRANSISCO, CALIFORNIA 94104

April 1, 1982

Mr. Prentiss Robert Jackson
27 Cornfeld Hall
The Business School
Boston, Massachusetts 02163

Dear Mr. Jackson:

Thank you for forwarding to me your letter and resume regarding a position with us.

As you may be aware, we only hire an associate once every several years, and have received letters from an enormous number of interested applicants. As a result, it is just not possible for us to speak with all qualified candidates. This requires that we make difficult decisions based on extremely limited information with respect to the personality and qualifications of each candidate. While we were impressed with your credentials, we regretfully will not be able to invite you to meet with us at this time.

We would, however, like to thank you for your interest in venture capital and in Croesus Partners, and will hold your resume in our files for consideration in the future.

Sincerely,

Thaddeus J. Wheeler
General Partner

WHAT THE COMPANY REALLY MEANT:

CROESUS PARTNERS
VULTURE CAPITAL
SUITE 900
EMBARCADERO AT THE FAULT LINE
SAN FRANSISCO, CALIFORNIA 94104

April 1, 1982

Mr. Prentiss Robert Jackson
27 Cornfeld Hall
The Business School
Boston, Massachusetts 02163

Dear Mr. Jackson:

Our compliments-- that resume looks pretty sharp. You
Business School types know all the tricks-- the bold type,
justified margins, ivory laid paper, even stamping the
envelope <u>confidential</u> to distinguish it from the rest of our
junk mail.

Our business is people and cutting high-tech deals: at
Croesus Partners we fail to see how being a reconstructed
short-order chicken cook qualifies you for the high-rolling
world of venture capital.

But over the years, we've learned it doesn't pay to
insult lightweights from big-name business schools. Today's
job reject may be the president of tomorrow's Federal
Express, or might oppose us in a leveraged buy-out out of
pure vindictiveness. We hope this personalized letter of
concern dashed off by our Wang 145 will pacify you.

Sincerely,

Thaddeus J. Wheeler
Thaddeus J. Wheeler
General Partner

P.S. Though we can't offer you a job,
we might be willing to pick up your
second year tuition expenses in return
for an 80% contingent interest on your
future income stream.

How to Answer the Ten Most Loaded Interviewing Questions: A Self-Teaching Quiz

1. Why did you major in fine arts instead of something more practical . . . like accounting?

(a) I knew I was headed for a business career even back then, but felt—and still feel—that it is important to be a well-rounded individual.

(b) (Sobbing:) I was young . . . foolish . . . easily misled.

(c) The social life was better in fine arts.

(d) I wanted to get in on the coming boom in pre-Columbian art.

2. Why did you leave your last job?

(a) There was no career potential for me there.

(b) My CETA grant expired.

(c) I was fired.

3. Why did you decide to get your M.B.A.?

(a) To lead the reindustrialization of America.

(b) (Still sobbing:) I was young . . . foolish . . . easily misled.

(c) If the government insisted on loaning me money at 7 percent to get a salary-doubling M.B.A., who was I to say no?

(d) Anything was better than working two more years at the bank.

4. Did you read the article about Wheelabrator-Frye's new acquisition in the last issue of *Business Week*?

(a) Didn't everybody?

(b) Yeah, but the real story was in April's *Financial Analyst's Journal*.

(c) No, I haven't subscribed to *Business Week* since they did that hatchet job on American industry in September.

(d) Wheelabrator-Frye? Aren't they the backup band for Fleetwood Mac?

5. How would you feel about eventually transferring to Corporate in New York?

(a) How good is your life insurance coverage?

(b) Well, I hear that studio apartments rent for $1,000 a month—but I figure on sleeping in the office anyway for the first couple of years.

(c) (Breaking into song:) I love New York!

(d) No problem—I minored in Spanish at college.

6. How would you feel about starting out for a few years in our stamping plant in Altoona, Pennsylvania?

(a) Whatever is best for the company.

(b) Great, I love big cities.

(c) Okay, okay, I'll take 10 percent less!

(d) Can you pick up all three networks there?

7. As a woman entering the corporate world, what are your plans for raising a family?

(a) My husband is willing to stay home and take care of the kids.

(b) I plan to have a girl in 1986 after making assistant vice-president, and a boy in 1989 after making senior V.P. I'll play it by ear from there.

(c) Would you lean a little closer to the microphone before repeating that question?

8. Bob, are you ready to roll up your sleeves and take orders for eighty hours a week at our firm?

(a) I guess you have to pay your dues in any great company.

(b) Sounds like a piece of cake after business school.

(c) Does Illinois have no-fault divorce?

(d) Let's see, $45,000 divided by eighty hours divided by fifty-two weeks is . . .

9. Given your past experience, what kind of salary would you expect from this job?
(a) Oh, anything in the $20,000 to $50,000 range.
(b) Salary is really secondary to challenge and personal growth in my consideration of job opportunities.
(c) How about minimum wage?
(d) Whatever you offer, plus 20 percent.

10. What would you say if I offered you a job right this minute?
(a) Let me get back to you in fifteen minutes. I don't believe in deciding important issues on short notice.
(b) Gee, I'm flattered by your offer, but I really came down here this morning just to brush up on my interview skills before talking with IBM next week.
(c) Fantastic. Your offer will be worth at least $5,000 in my salary bargaining with Digital Datawhack.

I Walked Into My Interview Cold—

AN APPLICANT'S *TRUE CONFESSION*

"So, Mr. Elbert, why do you want to work for us?"

I eyed the man across from me intently. With his gray suit and red tie, he could have passed for a consultant. Wait a second, I thought with a chill, maybe he is a consultant. It was then that the terrible truth dawned on me: I'd forgotten to look at the name on the door of the interview booth. I squirmed and turned pale. I'd been granted interviews by over fifty big corporations and professional firms; which one was this?

"I say, Mr. Elbert, why do you want to work for us?"

I refused to let my composure be shattered. Two years at business school had taught me never to shy away from subjects I knew nothing about. I looked up and smiled. "Why would anyone with my interests want to work for you? Because you're one of the real innovators in the industry, that's why!" My smile stretched from ear to ear now. "And I hear it's a great place for an M.B.A. to work."

The man's face grew cold, quizzical. "An innovator? To be honest, I've never heard us called that before."

The pieces started to fit together. Not an innovator; clearly, the company must be in a slow-moving industry, like coal mining or steel.

His eyes narrowed. "Perhaps you'd like to tell me your qualifications for the position."

Coal mining or steel. That probably meant being a foreman in a plant somewhere. I made my voice icy calm. "My primary qualifications stem from my navy training. I have a great deal of experience supervising men."

"Supervising men?" He looked incredulous. "But you must know that in our firm it will be at least three years before you're promoted from management trainee."

Damn, I thought. What could it be? Maybe it was that off-the-wall job with a TV station I had written to. It was worth a try.

"You will notice on my résumé that I have extensive experience as a submarine communicator. That would undoubtedly be useful to you."

"Useful?" he said with disbelief. There was silence. It grew oppressive. Marshaling all my resources, I started to laundry-list my abilities:

"I can write songs." Silence . . .

Nix advertising and CBS Records.

"I'm a qualified color TV repairman." Silence . . .

Forget Intel and Sony.

"I speak some Norwegian and French." Silence . . .

Cross out Scandinavian Lines and Coty.

"I can read upside down in a mirror." Silence . . .

Drop the Rand Corporation.

"I've never written a bad check." Silence . . .

Clearly not Chrysler.

"I don't like coffee."

Silence . . .

Not even the Pancreas Foundation.

"I've developed a new-concept computer model that forecasts stock prices with unprecedented accuracy."

The man leaned forward, suddenly intense. "Fascinating. And what was the first thing your model told you to do."

I smiled. "Sell Exxon short."

He beamed. "Mr. Elbert, you've got the job. Give my office a call tomorrow and we'll work out the details."

I shook his hand and left, too embarrassed to ask who had hired me. Now it was too late to find out. Oh, well, perhaps there would be other job offers. But never again would I dare to enter an interview *cold!*

Strategic Wardrobe Management

CLOTHING IS UNDENIABLY a key success factor in business. If it weren't, naked people no doubt would figure more prominently in corporate society. Though just wearing clothes gives you an

"Mr. Gorman, you look like a million dollars, such as it looks today."

x

134

enormous leg up on those who don't, the wise M.B.A. soon learns that strategic dressing techniques make all the difference between a career in the fast track and one in the breakdown lane.

Fashion designers and clothing salespeople forever trill clothing as a vehicle for self-expression. But when it comes to business dress, don't believe it. All manuals for successful business dress prescribe a conservative and highly standardized uniform, although minor variations are allowable for some subcultures of the business world.

Briefly stated, the "M.B.A. look" for men consists of solid navy blue or gray suits, or occasionally pinstripes for a touch of splash.* For truly daring summer wear—seersucker. Your shirts can be any color as long as they're blue or white, made of Oxford cloth, and neatly

pressed before wear. Ties should be understated patterns or rep stripes in colors that appear in nature. Shoes should be black or dark brown and well shined. Studiously avoid shoes with stacked heels, buckles, or two-tone designs.

Another way to define the right look is by saying what it is *not*. The best example of how *not* to dress for business is what is known as the "Full Cleveland." The Full Cleveland consists of a dark blue or brown short-sleeved shirt,

The full Cleveland.

---

* Women have a little more freedom in their business dress—but not much. See the "Women in Business" chapter.

a white polyester tie, white patent-leather belt, and white patent-leather slip-on shoes. Wear the Full Cleveland, and your corporation may condemn you to living there.

Recently, the fashion press has coined the phrase *investment clothing.* One's wardrobe, after all, is nothing more than a portfolio of apparel investments. It is helpful to think of your clothes the same way you think of your stocks and bonds: some are the high fliers of the moment, while others need to be deep-sixed. Divest yourself of that tie your grandmother gave you two Christmases ago, and expand your position in low-beta button-down shirts.

Let's face it, by now everyone in business from the mail clerks on up has read John T. Molloy's treatise *Dress for Success.* This monograph was a landmark for its time. But merely learning how to choose the right business fabrics, or selecting the patterns in a tie, is not enough anymore. Everyone

now has the basic uniform of business pretty much figured out: the battleground for sartorial dominance is shifting to the more subtle insignias of rank—the *power accessories.* For the first time anywhere, we offer a compendium of M.B.A. power accessories.

Power Accessory No. 1: The Attaché Case

The single most important accessory item for any aspiring executive is the leather lunch pail, or attaché case. This accessory more than any other identifies you as a *decision maker.* It is wise to begin carrying such a case early in your career, even if the only decision authority you have is setting the darkness control on the office copier . . . and the only thing you carry in it is your lunch.

The attaché case is one of the few business accoutrements for which bigger is *not* better—only the

Attaché Cases (from bottom): (a) **The ultimate.** *Italian leather exterior and interior, brass corners and locks, elegant styling. A very thin case. About $425. (b)* **Passes muster.** *Brown leather sides and handles, leather exterior but fabric inside. Elegant, but slightly bulkier. $280. (c)* **Good for starters.** *Exterior of high-impact plastic, locks chrome-plated. Often confused with a typewriter case. $75. (d)* **The Third World case.** *Expensive, but a little too loud. $320.*

minions carry accordion-style cases large enough to lug a full set of the *Encyclopaedia Britannica.* Upper-level decision makers deal only in one-page memos.

Choosing just the right case requires great care. We suggest cases that are made of genuine belting leather, simple in design, of rigid frame construction, in dark brown. Your monogram should be affixed modestly on the case with burned-in letters—not gold—not exceeding ⅜ inch high.

Though purchase of a suitable attaché case early in one's career is recommended, the rising cost of fine leather may force you to forgo immediate purchase. If you insist on allocating your tight budget to necessities like food and shelter first, you must at least carry a folded copy of the *Wall Street Journal* to and from work to signal your daily communion with Mammon.

Warning: When shopping for your first attaché case, it is imperative never to ask inadvertently for a briefcase, lest the salespeople mistake you for a lawyer.

Power Accessory No. 2: The Electronic Calculator

Next to the attaché case, the electronic calculator is the most essential executive appendage. In ten short years the calculator has taken the business world by storm. In fact, the tenfold expansion of newly minted M.B.A.'s in the past decade is largely the result of the advent of the multifunction business calculator. Only after the introduction of a hand-held machine that could magically perform regression analysis, linear programming, and internal rate of return was it possible for hordes of otherwise unemployable English majors and philosophy jocks to survive the quantitative rigors of business school.

These days any Cub Scout with a sixth-grade mastery of arithmetic can calculate the imputed cost of capital of a multimillion-dollar sale/leaseback deal in seconds. But don't think that massaging your calculator is just a way of eking out a six-figure salary. In addition to being a ready source of corporate analysis, the calculator is often a one-way ticket to financial fantasyland. That executive across the table from you furiously pounding the keys of her Texas Instruments M.B.A. is just as apt to be calculating the appreciation of her condo as grinding out this month's marketing forecast.

If you look hard enough,

The Calculator (left to right): (a) **The Texas Instruments M.B.A.** *A good beginner's model. Includes compound interest capability, statistics, and limited programmability. Probably the cheapest and quickest way to get your degree. $60. (b)* **The Sharp PC-1211 pocket computer** *(with CE-122 printer). Whoa! Has a complete set of alphabet keys for those who are not content with pushing only numbers. About $310. (c)* **The HP-12C.** *Introduced in 1981, it is rapidly becoming the standard product for connoisseurs. In addition to standard features offered by competitors, the 12C includes built-in depreciation functions and sophisticated bond yield calculations. $150. (d)* **The Astro.** *A four-function specialist's machine that also casts horoscopes. Used primarily by technical stock market analysts. $45.*

you can find calculators that can do anything from playing a Bach fugue to plotting biorhythms. But truly executive calculators are strictly business. Who needs music when you can crunch net present values to the tune of seven figures? Who needs biorhythms to tell you this was the wrong day to get out of bed when your HP12-C tells you that the new 23 percent prime rate has shipwrecked your latest expansion plans?

We suggest carrying a spare calculator with you at all times. There's nothing more embarrassing than having your number-one unit go down at an important business meeting and having to admit you've forgotten how to do long division. If that dread day should occur, there's only one solution: make up numbers out of whole cloth and talk extremely rapidly. Chances are your boss won't understand what you're talking about anyway.

Power Accessory No. 3: The Executive Appointment Book

An inexpensive but very powerful executive accessory is the pocket diary or appointment book. This is the clearinghouse for all major meetings, luncheon dates, hair appointments, golf games, and other events. Disciplined use of this book will do much to improve your efficient time management. More important, *conspicuous* consultation of your pocket diary will do much to make you look the part of the sought-after, time-pressured *decision maker.*

There are various makes of these diaries, ranging from the "little black book" to full-blown desktop models. The best are those that combine the appointment function with the phone-and-address function. Some even have a pen holder right in the book so that you are never at a loss for a writing instrument. The entry-level appointment book is usually spiral-bound and made of vinyl or Naugahyde. But for executives who demand accessories with maximum firepower, we suggest the leather-bound pocket diary by Mark Cross.

The executive diary has several other important functions. It is the reference book of last resort when you want to duck an undesired invitation, as in "I hate to ask for a rain check, but I'm afraid I'm booked solid until a year from November." The diary also makes a good doodling pad when you are bored. Finally, it is probably the only way to figure out at the end of the year what the hell you did during the previous twelve months.

*Appointment Books (front row, left to right): (a) **Leatherette.** $8.50. (b) **Vinyl.** $3.50. (c) **Paper.** The Robinson Road Reminder for traveling salesmen. Note that the cover of the 1982 edition still displays cars from the heyday of American business. $1.50. (back row): (d) **Genuine leather,** from Mark Cross. Contains an address booklet and quarterly inserts with a full page provided for each day, allowing detailed appointment making for important times of the year. $100.*

Power Accessory No. 4: The Tropical Tan

A few business people come by their tans honestly. They manage to schedule industry conferences in the islands during February or can afford to take sun-filled family vacations to Cancún. But, as with every other power accessory from Guccis to Savile Row suits, the hon-est tan has its more accessible imitators. If you have ever wondered how so many stiffs in your office achieve the year-round tan, one thing's for sure: it's not from the fluorescent glare of their desk lamps. Smart money says they use a sunlamp on the sly.

The sunlamp allows even the most harried business types to radiate a deep tan all year long, vacations or no. But the year-round tan is recommended for senior managers only; too much color can be problematic for junior execs. To look anything but sallow during your first few years in the bullpen might give your superiors the impression they have not been keeping you busy enough during weekends. But if you insist on seeking a tan with your sunlamp, or alternatively at an indoor tanning spa, we can offer a few suggestions:

1. Use a sunlamp only on weekends. That way, if the office wise guy remarks on the sudden appearance of your tan, you can fabricate some story about a sun-stroked weekend at some island Shangri-La

like Caneel Bay. Nothing is more transparent than leaving the office at 11:45 on a Tuesday night, only to return an Aztec sun god at 8:15 the next morning.

2. During the winter, wear ski goggles while lying under the lamp. The white area around your eyes will help corroborate your story of having spent the weekend schussing through nine inches of fresh powder.

Warning: Excessive use of your sunlamp beyond maximum suggested exposure times can lead to premature executive burnout.

Power Accessory No. 5: The Business Card

The business card is a concise statement of your corporate identity. It lists your name, firm, business address, title, and telephone number. The style of the card depends greatly on the business you are in, but a few general words of caution are appropriate here:

1. Avoid overly pretentious job titles such as "Lord of the Realm, Defender of the Faith, Emperor of India" or "Director of Corporate Planning."

2. Exercise modesty in choosing the printed size of your name.

3. Engraved cards radiate more power than letterpress cards. Letterpress cards radiate more power than offset cards.

4. Stick with heavy 100 percent rag white or ecru stock and standard ink colors.

5. Steer clear of trite business slogans, like "Our Business Is Always Picking Up" for a refuse service.

6. Omit your home telephone number if you enjoy being married.

The style in which you present your card is also crucial. Many young executives new to the game are so proud of having that first card that they dispense it the way new fathers dispense cigars, spitting them out with the speed and dexterity of a top dealer from Vegas. This is bad form. Wait until the conclusion of a business discussion to exchange cards. That way you can give the card that personalized touch—such as writing down the price of your product, giving out your private number at the office, or scribbling your secret Swiss bank account number.

Power Accessory No. 6: The Executive Pen

Because the pen is mightier than the sword, it is advisable to choose your weapon with great care. Nothing will dash your cultivated image of business polish more quickly than cutting a billion-dollar debt deal with a half-chewed Bic Banana.

The most-favored pens among executives still are the trim metal ball-points sheathed in plated gold or silver by Cross. It is remarkable how inexpensive these starter pens are, usually obtainable as a pen-and-pencil set for $25 to $75. Many corporations, in fact, issue their executives sets of these pens with the corporate logo inscribed, rather than risk having their employees be seen with stubby pencils, disposable products, or quills.

Because of the enormous popularity of the Cross pen during the past two decades, the corporate cognoscenti have been forced to

The Executive Pen (left to right): (a) **The Cross.** *Standard issue. Sterling silver, $35. (b)* **The Schaeffer Targa** *fountain pen, with woodgrained barrel. A good desk model, but a little heavy to lug around. $120. (c)* **The Elsa Peretti.** *The classic for executive women. Sterling silver, about $35. (d)* **The Montblanc** *fountain pen, from West Germany. 14-karat gold barrel, 18-karat gold point. For executives with 24-karat gold egos. $180 to $6000. (e)* **The well-chewed felt-tip.** *Recommended for home use only. $0.79.*

flee up-market to the ultimate: the gold Mont Blanc fountain pen from West Germany for men ($180 and up) and the silver Elsa Peretti for women (about $35).

Be wary of offbeat or bohemian ink colors like red, green, or brown; hard-hitting business types go for black and blue (dark only).

Pens should be placed carefully in your briefcase *(sic)* or inside jacket. At all costs, avoid the plastic shirt-pocket insert worn by engineers and TV repairmen. Do not abuse your pens by chewing them in public or nervously playing the "Wipeout" drum solo during board meetings. If you have to use your pen to cover up the butterflies, tap it lightly on your cheek while looking thoughtful. It will make others think you are generating very deep corporate strategy.

Power Accessory No. 7: The Handbag (for Women Only)

Many books (including *The Women's Dress for*

Success Book) have suggested that the well-dressed woman executive eschew the use of a handbag. Obviously, the author of that book was not a woman. Where else is a female executive to carry her hairbrush, her wallet, her checkbook, her sunglasses, her contact-lens case, her keys, her makeup case (containing eye shadow, mascara, blusher, lipstick, crayon kohl, and compact), her pillbox, her Band-Aids, her credit cards, her spray can of Mace, her nail file, her spare L'eggs, her Maalox, her black book, her whistle, and a paperback to read on the way to work? Certainly not in her attaché case: having a pair of spare nylons fall out when rummaging for your calculator and quarterly pro-formas during a divisional marketing meeting just doesn't wash.

The properly dressed businesswoman should carry her professional tools in an attaché case (same as the male case, although occasionally smaller or less clumsy) and her personal belongings in a handbag. But be careful to keep the size and weight of the bag reasonable: a 110-pound female executive constantly schlepping a 15-pound business case in one hand and a 35-pound handbag in the other is apt to take on the appearance of a Times Square bag lady.

The proper handbag for women execs should be of natural leather or designer canvas in dark or neutral colors. It should drape comfortably over the shoulder and hang unobtrusively under the arm. Avoid gold lamé evening bags and bags made from the skins of endangered species like kangaroos, alligators, or male chauvinist pigs.

Power Accessory No. 8: The Signature

The three most important words you will ever write as a business executive—and eventually the *only* words you will ever physically write yourself as a senior executive—are your first, middle, and last names. Your signature is

EVOLUTION OF AN
EXECUTIVE
SIGNATURE

Year		Career station
1931	*alfie*	Hired as stock boy at sixteen. Not allowed to sign anything but receiving reports. Circle over the *i* draws rude comments from delivering truckers.
1937	*al Stern*	Promoted to salesman. Adds last name to make contracts legal and new nickname to make customers think he's a good ol' boy.
1939	*alfred Stern*	Promoted to sales manager. Switches to full first name to add dignity. Signature still somewhat legible, but evinces more maturity and determination. Clearly a man to watch.
1947	*a. Franklin Stern*	After returning from aircraft-carrier duty in Pacific is promoted to vice-president of sales. Use of middle name reflects secret ambition to seek company presidency.
1959	*a. F St—*	Promoted to executive vice-president. Uses first initials only to save precious time; legibility decreases correspondingly.
1969	*AFS*	President. Traveling light—initials only. Growth in size of signature directly proportional to growth in ego.
1981	*scrawl*	Chairman of the board. Returns to his full signature now that he has more "quiet time." Scrawl now completely illegible. Often confused with his electrocardiogram.

your personal logo and deserves careful evaluation and occasional modification. An impressive John Hancock is good career insurance: a proper signature should express an executive's drive, energy, and sensitivity to his or her station in the corporate hierarchy.

Your signature must

evolve constantly through your career. An inscrutably illegible signature is considered pretentious for a junior executive, whereas an artlessly legible signature is considered immature in a high-through-put paper pusher. To avoid confusion, it may be helpful to trace the life cycle of an executive's signature, that of Alfred Franklin Stern.

Power Accessory No. 9: The Credit Card

The successful businessman used to be thought of as someone who would pay for an expensive business luncheon by pulling out his money clip and extracting a wad of $50 and $100 bills. No longer: carrying rolls of greenbacks is not only unsafe and unprofessional—it's passé. Try renting a car from Hertz with cash, and you'll be treated like a drifter if you can't produce plastic.

But how to start? How can you qualify for that first card when the only credit you've ever received consists of an account from a campus bookstore and $20 you still owe the phone company?

The answer is to start building your credit-card collection modestly. An application blitz of department stores and major oil companies will always yield a few cards. Granted, credit from Sunoco won't even buy you dinner at Howard Johnson's—but it *will* (along with a few months of solid work experience and a positive bank balance) leverage you up to the next tier of plastic, MasterCard and Visa, or even to an American Express green.

From there it's all up to you. A few years of drive, hard work, and luck can qualify you for the trump card of credit, the Amex Gold. If you are new to the game and are unfamiliar with the proper use of credit cards—when to hold 'em, when to fold 'em— please refer to the following guide.

CREDIT CARD
ETIQUETTE

1. If you must use minor-league plastic like MasterCard or Visa at a restaurant, don't let your business associates know. Quietly extract it from your wallet while pretending to check the addition of the bill. Then you can hand bill and card to the waiter together without betraying your embarrassingly weak hand.

By contrast, if you have a real power card like a Sears Platinum or Amex Gold, quietly play it face up with polished insouciance.

2. Beware of friends who offer to pick up the tab on their cards, while asking you to reimburse them for your share in cash. Their motives may be less than magnanimous. With interest rates around 20 percent, the free use of your half, plus his ability to sit on the bill for sixty days until it comes due, will yield him an annualized return of nearly 30 percent, *after taxes!* This gambit is currently the rage among money managers on Wall Street, most of whom can't manage *pretax* yields of more than 17 or 18 percent from conventional investments like stocks or bonds.

3. If you are caught short at a business meeting without a prestige card, *never* admit it. Reach *slowly* for your wallet, allowing your companions to get their cards out first. Alternatively, preempt the competition with a declaration like "I don't believe in plastic money. The explosion in consumer credit is turning the American economy into a house of MasterCards."

4. The best investment of all is actually to pay cash but to demand a 3 or 4 percent *discount* from the restaurant or hotel. Remember, business establishments pay credit-card companies 4 to 7 percent off the top on all charges; they should be willing to cut you in on the extra profits they earn by accepting cash. If they object, remind them that dollar bills are still legal tender backed by the full faith and credit of the United States Treasury and are accepted in over fifty million retail establishments throughout the world.

5. Be careful not to overextend yourself. The *Wall Street Journal* recently carried a story about a young man who obtained over 1,500 credit cards, carrying a combined credit line in excess of $1.5 million; his annual salary was $14,000. Imagine how well you could do.

4

TRICKS OF THE TRADE

Office Politics and Etiquette

IN THE REAL WORLD, THE only thing that counts is performance—recent performance. Anything that happened before the close of the last quarter is ancient history. But while cutting costs, increasing market share, reducing employee turnover, and shut-

"I like the way you push, Dodds. Pushers eventually become movers and shakers."

ting out the opposition in office softball are tangible measures of performance, they are not enough. To a large extent, when a corporation evaluates executive performance, *perception is reality.* You have to project the right image at all times if you want to rise above second-rank jobs like vice-president.

Lesson One: Moving and Shaking

First impressions are important. The handshake is your first line of offense when meeting clients or colleagues. There are many types of handshakes used in business, and it is important to master as many of them as possible. Consult the following guide to expand your repertoire and improve your ability to "read" the handshakes you receive.

1. The Straight Shake

Hands meet fully extended, lock, and clasp with moderate strength for no more than three seconds. This classic shake, developed after long hours of practice, is the international standard for businessmen everywhere.

2. The Twofer Shake

This hearty shake is the favorite of enthusiastic types, like salesmen and real estate promoters. The trick here is to reinforce the straight shake (above) with a blind-side attack by the left hand. Also used often by drunken acquaintances at national conventions—especially when they're trying to weasel a job or a contract out of you.

3. The Shakedown

The shakedown is the hallmark of jovial ex-athletes or self-made millionaires who tend to regard every introduction as an opportunity for hand-to-hand combat. It is similar to the straight shake except for the intensity of application and the more extended duration. To perform this shake, first work out for several months with a wrist exerciser. Give your opponent a solid six-count before delivering the release.

4. The Golden Handshake

This one is particularly effective when dealing with foreign governments, local politicians, or FBI agents posing as Middle Eastern oil sheiks.

5. The Soul Shake

Use this shake when you really want to break the ice at board meetings or job interviews. It's also helpful when you desire to show contemporaries you haven't lost that 1960s anti-establishment spirit— even though you recently voted for Ronald Reagan.

Other Options

Those who find the handshake needlessly for-

mal occasionally opt for an embrace, a kiss on both cheeks, or a pat on the back. The embrace or kiss should be used advisedly, but is safe in France and other developing nations. Women executives are constantly confronted with male counterparts who are unsure of whether to kiss, shake, or use an alternate technique. If you do not want to be kissed, put out your hand when your opponent is at least five feet away and offer him the straight shake. If he ignores your signals and tries to kiss anyway, stop him cold with a bone-crushing shakedown.

Each of these variant techniques has its place in the business world. If you find yourself in unfamiliar surroundings or are in any doubt whatsoever, opt for the low-risk strategy and deliver the straight shake.

Lesson Two: How to Make the Right Small Talk

Small talk is important: it's bad form to be

caught with nothing to say. But if you want to impress your business associates, it's a good idea to be able to utter sentences slightly more sophisticated than "Nice day if it don't rain." That requires practice and careful study.

The first rule of business conversation is: don't sound too intellectual. It's okay to dabble in subjects other than business, as long as you don't bore others with monologues on topics like the dialectic in Freudian analysis, Eastern religions, or *The Effect of Gamma Rays on Man-in-the-Moon Marigolds.* The house intellectual is always regarded with suspicion in business. Not as a threat, exactly—just faintly unreliable.

No one is saying that as a consenting adult you can't be concerned with such things in the privacy of your own home. But only on a few public occasions—such as gallery openings or when having drinks with your CEO's artist wife—will you want to trot out your ability to sound *au courant.* The

boss's wife will think you're fun and invite you back. If you're ever interviewed by the press, the ability to drop high-sounding phrases will earn you kudos as "a far-sighted and creative business leader." You will be invited to join the boards of art museums populated by other far-sighted and creative business leaders.

In short, sounding intellectual in business is about as acceptable as openly talking about making a buck if you're a college professor. Confine your speech to discussion of the weather, last weekend, this weekend, parking tickets, the spouse and kids, wine, vacations (anybody's), the Fed's monetary policy, the evils of "progressive" taxation, residential real estate prices, and good movies you've seen lately (if you can think of any). Articles in the *Wall Street Journal* or *Sports Illustrated* are always good bets. Avoid mentioning subjects like your ex-spouse and kids, the imminent domination of your industry by the Japanese, controlled substances, your salary, and the meaning of corporate life.

Acceptable Books to Say You've Read: Suspense novels by Robert Ludlum. Cultural biopsies by Tom Wolfe. Apocalyptic financial novels by Paul Erdman, including *The Crash of '79*, *The Billion Dollar Sure Thing*, and *The Last Days of America*. James Michener. Herman Wouk's *The Winds of War*. Anything on the Civil War. Anything on the rise of the Rockefellers, Vanderbilts, or Mellons. *The Wealth of Nations* and *The Money Game*, both by Adam Smith.

Unacceptable Books to Say You've Read: Anything by Barry Commoner. *The Female Eunuch* by Germaine Greer. *Das Kapital* by Karl Marx. *Baby and Child Care* by Benjamin Spock. There are also some self-help books that you should make a point of reading—but never admit to, lest your colleagues get the idea that you didn't come by your business savvy naturally. These include: *Power* and *Success* by Michael Korda, *Winning Through Intimidation* by Robert Ringer, and *Competitive Strategy* by Michael E. Porter.

Acceptable Intellectuals: Dale Carnegie, Milton Friedman, Malcolm Forbes, Phil Donahue, Jack Kemp, William F. Buckley, Jr., Ayn Rand, and Casey Stengel.

Unacceptable Intellectuals: John Kenneth Galbraith, Shana Alexander, Ralph Nader, Jerry Brown, Christopher Lasch, Barry Manilow.

Acceptable Nonbusiness Magazines to Display on Your Coffee Table: *Time*, *National Geographic*, *Sports Illustrated*, *Savvy*, *Architectural Digest* (say your spouse gets it), *The New Yorker* (you get it for cartoons), *Sail*.

Unacceptable Magazines to Display on Your Coffee Table: *High Times*, *The Village Voice*, *Mother Jones*, *Cosmo*, *Consumer Reports*, *New Republic*. The ultimate *faux pas*: *Gentleman's Quarterly*.

THE WRITE STUFF: A GUIDE TO BUSINESS PUBLICATIONS

After you leave business school (or finish this book), it is important to keep current with things like the latest management theories, new tax angles, which conglomerate is swallowing which, who is the latest president of Occidental Petroleum, and other information. The following business publications are essential:

1. The Wall Street Journal. The daily Bible. Concentrate on the features in columns one, four, and six of the front page, and the stock listings inside the back cover. The *Journal* is preferable to the *Times* for the harried business person, because it distills all important world news into one front-page column.

World War Three, if it ever comes, will merit only a four-line mention here (with a reference to an inside feature de-

scribing the war's impact on cocoa futures).

2. Business Week. Generally boring, but you should at least glance through the table of contents to see if *your* company is profiled this week. The quantitative magazine for middle managers, *BW* always puts juicy titles on tedious articles like "Corporate Scoreboard: Third-Quarter Profits Fatten as Margins Slim" or "Spain: A Labor Subsidy Perils the Social Contract."

3. Forbes. Similar to *BW* but has more accessible writing and the entertaining weekly column

"Fact and Comment" by Chairman Malcolm Forbes. Look in the back for weekly columns by market analysts like Heinz Biel, David Dremen, and (occasionally) Andrew Tobias. Good cover art.

4. Barron's. Business's weekly tabloid. But unlike rival tabloids, which feature stories like "I Dated Frank Sinatra," *Barron's* counters with weekly

cover gossip by the Rona Barrett of Wall Street, Alan Abelson. *Barron's* is also known for having forty or so pages of the most complete over-the-counter stock listings available anywhere.

5. Fortune. Sister publication to *Life* and *Money*, features beautiful color photographic essays on meat-packing plants and strip mines. It costs a fortune, too ($2.50 an issue, biweekly). The home of the famous Fortune 500, Second 500, and International 500; also the home of frequent 500-page advertising inserts like "Brazil: Land of Mucho Dollars," paid for by

every developing nation that wants to blow its horn or roll over its loans from Citibank.

6. Inc. and **Venture.** Monthlies for the small businessman or would-be entrepreneur. Look for the rival Inc. 100 every spring (the 100 "fastest-growing small companies in America," *small* being defined as having sales of less than about $100 million a year). These publications feature topical articles like "Funeral Parlors: Franchise Opportunity of the Eighties."

Lesson Three: Dialing for Dollars (Executive Telephony)

Now that you are armed with the knowledge of what to talk *about*, it's important to focus on the medium through which many of your business conversations will be held: the telephone. Alexander Graham Bell's invention puts every executive within a finger's reach of every other executive. This ease of access is a true boon if you are trying to sell life insurance, but a true bane if you are the unhappy recipient of such unsolicited or undesired phone calls.

Executive telephony is the body of elaborate strategies executives use to screen unwanted calls and the equally elaborate countervailing strategies used to penetrate an opponent's expert screening.

Defensive Strategies

1. Instruct your secretary to obtain the name and company of the caller and the purpose of the call.
2. Have the secretary relay the information to you. Determine whether the call is to be put through or "terminated with extreme prejudice."

"I'm sorry—he's shoveling funds into offshore accounts at the moment."

3. If the call is from an irate creditor, the Patrolman's Benevolent Association, or your mother-in-law, have your secretary respond with one of the following defensive misrepresentations:

(a) "Ms. Stratemeyer is away from her desk."

(b) "Ms. Stratemeyer is in conference."

(c) "Ms. Stratemeyer has left for the day."

(d) "Ms. Stratemeyer no longer works here."

(e) "I'm sorry, Ms. Stratemeyer died after a long bout with jet lag last week."

If you are the intended victim of one of these calls and do not want to mortally offend the caller, it's a good idea to call back at a time such as 1:15 in the afternoon—when it is a virtual certainty that your caller will be away at lunch. Leave a message that you returned the call . . . and instruct your secretary to use a different defensive strategy when the caller calls again after lunch.

Offensive Strategies

Not so many years ago, you could always get a secretary to put your call through to her boss simply by telling her that you were calling long distance. This gambit is all but obsolete today, thanks to the advent of WATS lines and 800 numbers. The current way to punch through telephonic defenses is to imply vaguely that your call is of utmost importance. Use a plausible fiction like "It's about the proposed merger . . . a billion bucks are at stake." If someone owes you thousands of dollars and you haven't been able to penetrate his defensive perimeter for months, we suggest trying a high-risk strategy such as passing yourself off as a medical doctor. "Hello, this is Dr. Ryan at Mother of Mercy Hospital. I'm calling about Mr. Walton's mother." Or in the last extremity: "This is Mr. Walton's broker. I've got some bad news and it's imperative that I speak to him before the market closes."

Hanging Up

The most difficult maneuver next to placing a business call successfully —or deflecting one—is ending one. You don't have to be a mullah of time management to know that marathon phone calls are public enemy number one when it comes to American white-collar productivity. Just because the other guy on the line has nothing better to do than recite last night's Carson monologue or rail against the nine-digit zip code doesn't mean you are obliged to stay on the line. If you are stuck on the line and getting desperate, it's always best to try for the *graceful* exit. But this is not always possible. The following is a list of the five most popular ways to get yourself off the hook, listed in decreasing order of politeness:

1. "Frank, I'd love to talk more, but I know you're a busy man so I'll let you go."
2. "Frank, that's my other line ringing. I hate to run, but let's talk again soon."
3. [Accompanied by groans of pain:] "Damn! My ulcers are acting up again. Sorry, Frank—got to run to the nurse's office for some Tagamet."
4. "Listen, there are several more urgent calls on my board—let me put you on low-priority hold."
5. Hang up in mid-sentence. When the caller calls back, have your secretary blame technological difficulties but say you were called away from the office on urgent business.

Lesson Four: Drink for Success

Though an occasional executive is heard to regret becoming a cog in a corporate machine, most executives find solace in knowing that corporate America is at least a *well-oiled* machine. Alcohol is a *sine qua non* of business life—a fact recently quantified by University of Chicago professors who determined that the prohibition of alcohol from 1920

to 1933 was the actual cause of the Great Depression.

Most business deals are conceived over a cocktail and closed on a cocktail napkin. In business or out before getting into bed with a total stranger, it helps to have a few drinks. Even if you are familiar with this basic scenario, it is wise to be aware of the rules that surround business drinking.

Rules of Successful Business Drinking

---

1. **Remember** that as a business executive, you are a *decision maker*. Abdicating responsibility by ordering a house brand of liquor shows that you are completely undiscriminating; it is tantamount to admitting you wear Jockey underwear. Better to affect savoir faire by ordering a Glenlivet on the rocks—especially when the bill comes and your drinking partners see that it cost you $6.50 a shot.

2. **Avoid** boozing before breakfast, except at conventions.

3. **Whenever** possible, plan your drinking assignments in advance and set a reasonable limit.

4. **Men should avoid** ordering the following during

the early going: Harvey Wallbanger, Zombie, Purple Jesus.

5. **Women should avoid** ordering the following drinks during the late going: double martini, Samoan War God, and Sloe Comfortable Screw (a concoction of sloe gin, Southern Comfort, and orange juice).

6. **American beers** are "in" after playing tennis or golf, when attending professional sports events, or when having a few after work. Foreign beers are *de rigueur* when attending artsy restaurants—and when on the road, assuming your meals are on an expense account. For executives who favor foreign beers but feel guilty about not buying American, try these "domestic imports": Tuborg (Carling), Erlanger (Schlitz), Würzburger (Anheuser-Busch), and Lowenbräu (Miller), all formerly brewed in Europe but now concocted or bottled in the good ol' U.S. of A.

7. **Always disdain** French wine in favor of the equivalent from California. Claim that it's "a better value."

8. **Trying to match the office lush** round for round will quickly convince you of the truth of Oscar Wilde's observation that "work is the curse of the drinking classes." A good rule of thumb: always drink less than your opposite number, especially when a slow negotiation turns into a marathon drinking session. If you are smart, you will be the first to switch to mineral water or Campari and soda.

9. **Some business types** —especially those hailing from places like Texas and Oklahoma—don't cotton to self-styled sophisticates whose idea of a good drink is a Dry Sack or a Lazy Sombrero. When you are caught between the Scylla of sobriety and the Charybdis of credibility, we suggest you order something with oomph like a double Jack Daniel's on the rocks —but nurse it slowly with plenty of ice.

Lesson Five: Business Air Travel

It may sound glamorous to travel to Denver one week, Chicago the next, and Atlanta the next, but for most business people, the traveling life very quickly becomes old. Fully 60 percent of all passenger air travel in the United States is done by businessmen on business trips. Only business travelers are in enough of a rush to subsidize the airlines by paying full fare instead of Supersaver; if corporations (and the IRS) hadn't created the expense account, we'd all be traveling by railroad.

Business air travel is significantly different from civilian travel. There are rules to follow on what kind of baggage to carry, how to act, etc.

"I hope you'll excuse me, but I couldn't help noticing. We both seem about to grab the same little company."

Do's and Don't's of Business Air Travel

1. **Do** fly first class—if you're on an expense account. You'll have more work space, you'll get somewhat edible food, and you'll be first off the plane. Besides, you get to meet more movers and shakers that way.

2. **Do not** ever check your baggage. Ever. It could get lost or stolen. Worst of all, it could cause you to miss your Detroit-Columbus connection. Any business traveler worth his salt can live for two or three weeks out of a single piece of carry-on luggage. That's why business travelers play tennis on their trips . . . and leave their golf clubs at home.

3. **Do** work on the plane instead of drinking too much booze and wasting time on vacuous airline magazines. This is especially true if you bill by the hour in your business, or if the person sitting next to you insists on showing you pictures of his grandchildren.

4. **Do not** work openly on top-secret company cost documents unless you have previously ascertained that the passenger next to you is blind, a rock musician on mood-ameliorating drugs, or the unfortunate possessor of a forty-seventh chromosome.

5. **Do** ante up the $50 a year to join at least one good airline club. Most people are not aware of it, but all big airports have somewhere far more comfortable to park yourself while waiting for a flight than those agonizing plastic airport chairs. If you've always wondered what hidden chamber all those first-class business passengers emerge from one minute before flight time, now you know.

6. **Do not** change your watch to local time when crossing time zones; you'll only get jet lag. Instead, especially on business trips of two days or less, try to eat meals and go to bed by your *home* time.

7. **Do** purchase airline insurance if you're scared

BUSINESS TRAVEL WITH STYLE

Some business people travel so often that they think nothing of taking a quick junket to a far-away city, just for the hell of it. We are familiar with one consulting team who had a meeting at their client's headquarters in Columbia, South Carolina, that didn't finish until 7:30 in the evening—far too late for them to make it home to New York on a scheduled flight. The four consultants had a choice: (a) Cool their heels in the Holiday Inn and bar in Columbia and fly back the next morning. Cost of hotels: $34 per night each, or $136 total. (b) Charter a Lear jet and fly home. Extra cost over first-class air fare: $1,950. (c) Fly to Washington, D.C., on the last flight of the day, stay at a first-class hotel, eat a ritzy dinner, and hit the hottest bars in Georgetown. Cost to client of extra hotels, meals, liquor, and other entertainment: $650. The consultants analyzed carefully, decided they couldn't justify the $1,950 just to spend the night with their families, and flew to Washington. They enjoyed themselves immensely, considered their decision a reasonable compromise, and billed the client $650.

of flying. It may be the worst insurance buy going, but thinking about that *tax-free* $300,000 will soothe your nerves when the airplane hits a sharp downdraft. Besides, when the insurance policy arrives in your home mail two days later, your spouse will know that you *really* care.

8. **Do not** waste time at the beginning of the flight watching the flight attendants do their safety spiel. If the plane crashes, you're a cooked goose anyway. And you'll always have a quick twenty seconds to put your Evelyn Wood training to work speed-reading the idiot card while the pilot tries to fly the plane on its one remaining engine.

9. **Do** ask for a second dinner on a partially empty flight. Usually they'll say no, but occasionally you'll get lucky and actually get to eat half your fill.

10. **Do not** try to pick up the flight attendants. Business has a bad enough public image these days

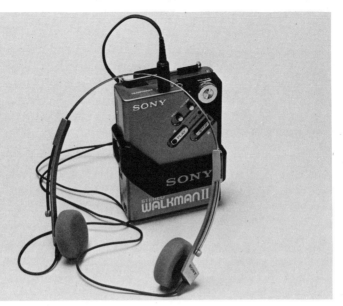

without your making it worse.

11. **Do** smile and say "thank you" to the flight attendants when deplaning. It's good practice for your upcoming business meetings.

Lesson Six: How to Survive Muzak

A major factor in the decline of America's productivity has been the introduction of supermarket music into the work environment. It's as if Americans don't get enough tunes from their car radios, home stereos, or Sony Walkmans. Muzak has gained in popularity during the past two decades, to the point where it's becoming inescapable. It is everywhere—washroom stalls, elevators, reception areas, and, most annoyingly, from the telephone when you are put on hold.

As innocuous as it sounds, Muzak is secretly an agent of subliminal mood control. Businesses buy it on the premise that efficiency is enhanced if workers are stimulated cyclically by emotional cli-

A Four-Piece Band in Three-Piece Suits

* * *

With Two Hit Albums,
  The MBA's Bring Their
  Message to America's
  Youth

By Barry Parr
Special to
The Wall Street Journal

NEW YORK—It wasn't all that long ago when a young business student at the London School of Economics, Mick Jagger, formed the Rolling Stones. Now four American M.B.A.'s—one from Harvard, two from Stanford, and one from Wharton—have started a new rock band, the MBA's, and are building a nationwide following among the upwardly mobile with haunting lyrics like:

We take our dates to expensive
  bars,
We own condominiums and
  drive fast cars,
Hey, hey, hey, we're the
  M.B.A.'s,
Can't you see we're the latest
  rage?
Having fun, making twice our
  age.

"We just felt it was time our generation started supporting the underdog," says the group's founder, Holden Gaines. "And who could be more of an underdog these days than American business?"

The group's free-spending fans couldn't agree more, and they've sent two of the group's tunes, "Résumé Mucho" and a protest number called "Take This Pink Slip and Beat It," to the top of the Fortune top 40. The MBA's' spare but telling lyrics have a unique ability to capture the raw emotional power of business life. When lead singer Holden Gaines belts out, "Come on, baby, merge with me—and feel that surge of synergy," administrative assistants scream tender offers at thirty times their earnings.

Their initial public offering, Fast Track, was an immediate success. Their latest album, White-Collar Blues, continues the style Wall Street Journal music critic Irving Kristol dubbed "neon conservative."

But not everyone in the business-music business is singing their praises. "Everything they say about these guys is true," declares Random Walker, pop-music analyst for Lehman Brothers. "They want it all now. They're not going to stick with a label for forty years so that they can get a gold record when they retire." Meanwhile, Variety has knocked the MBA's for being a "manufactured" band, calling them "the Prefab Four."

Undaunted by this criticism, the MBA's continue to bring their unique message to the world. When asked why a bunch of Street musicians were attracting such national media attention, Gaines answered with a shrug. "Anything can happen in a world where Greenwich Village is uptown."

maxes followed by productive plateaus. On Monday mornings, for example, the first segment usually starts off with an inspirational piece like "Theme from the FBI" or something with a back beat like "Satisfaction." This is followed by something people can actually work to, like the old Wayne Newton song "Bessie the Heifer." Now the office is really humming.

Muzak is generally found only where the challenge of the work is below sixth-grade level. If the top executives in your organization have Muzak piped into *their* office suites, it's time to sell your stock options short and give your notice. If Muzak is introduced into *your* area, there are basically four ways to cope: (a) earplugs (the best are made by the E.A.R. Corporation, 7911 Zionsville Road, Indianapolis, Indiana), (b) a white-noise generator, (c) your own radio with headphones, or (d) playing "Name That Tune" with the rest of the walking wounded. This is an office game suitable for all ages, since the anony-

mous horns and strings are so hungry for new material that they will homogenize beyond recognition anything from Hoagy Carmichael's "Stardust" to New Wave tunes like Devo's "Whip It."

Lesson Seven: Dealing With Data Processing

The greatest minds in business today are the IBM 3081, the Amdahl 470/V6, the Cray 1, and the Iliac IV. The specifications of these monster computers are staggering:

Speed: billions of calculations per second.

Memory: larger than the Library of Congress.

Input/output: 50 pages of printout per second.

Power consumption: 1 million watts and up.

Utilization: 23.73 hours per day (average).

Logic: binary.

Unfortunately, to harness the power of these machines, the average M.B.A. needs an interme-

GRANDON'S LAWS OF DATA PROCESSING

1. If one piece of valuable information is available from a computer, it will be contained in a 200-page printout.

2. Errors will be discovered in the accounting file only after the backup file has inadvertently been erased.

3. When a program prints detailed information, only the bottom line will be looked at.

4. When a program prints only the bottom line, detailed information will be sought.

5. Computer bugs are always discovered by the president of the company.

6. Computer security presents an impenetrable obstacle only to those who are supposed to use the system.

7. Just when you have become familiar with one computer system, the data-processing department will purchase an "updated" version.

8. The one day each month that the computer system goes down will be the one day you really need it.

9. Keypunching errors are never detected until after the check has been mailed.

10. Grandon's Inequality: the number of data processors + keypunchers + supervisors + maintenance personnel is always greater than the number of people the computer was brought in to replace.

diary—the data-processing specialist. Finding a DP specialist you can work with is a major problem, however: qualified DP personnel are in such demand that the one assigned to your department is likely to have the following specifications:

Speed: minimal.
Memory: about 10 percent of what he should know to do his job.
Input/output: About 70 spoken words per minute, 5 percent of which may be relevant.
Power consumption: 3,000 calories per day and up.
Utilization: approximately 22 hours a day of downtime, plus vacations, holidays, and retraining courses.
Logic: random.

Nevertheless, the movement toward the electronic office is one of the most important dynamics of our century. Every M.B.A. will have to reach his or her

own accommodation with the computer age. We suggest that if you can't beat 'em, join 'em. Subscribe to *BYTE* magazine. Learn how to use BASIC (a simple computer language) and Visicalc (an electronic spread sheet that can save you hours every day). Buy your own machine if you can afford it. (Apple and IBM desk-top microcomputers are becoming so prevalent in offices that they will be standard power accessories by the time the next edition of this book comes out.)

Lesson Eight: The Annual Office Christmas Party

For the young executive interested in rising quickly to the top, the annual Christmas party presents many risks and many opportunities. For particularly overbearing executives, it is the one chance during the year to shed their Scroogelike images and mingle casually with the support staff. It is also a time for your spouse to meet the boss's spouse, a time to mix with your colleagues from other departments, and a time to put on a skit that gently kids the company president with impunity.

The object here is to show your human side without seeming puerile. Be genial, but resist the temptation to let it all hang out. In many ways, the company Christmas party is a form of musical chairs played with one (or usually two) employees caught when the music stops, the subject of many hilarious stories for the rest of their working lives. Be on your guard: this is not the time to come out of the closet, break your college drinking record, or get caught *in flagrante delicto* under the office mistletoe.

Lesson Nine: The Annual Office Outing

It's eleven o'clock in the morning, June 28. You're out of raw materials. You

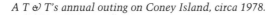

A T & T's annual outing on Coney Island, circa 1978.

call up the marketing vice-president of your largest supplier, but are told he's out. You ask for his assistant. She's out, too. You agree to settle for one of the product managers. *They're* not there either. In desperation you begin to name everyone you know in the company, and finally it dawns on you: you're out of luck. Nobody's in today —nobody at all. It must be the annual office outing.

The annual outing is generally held at the president's posh country club, in order to allow him to meet the staggering minimum guest charge quotas most such clubs require from their members. It is similar to the annual Christmas party, except that (a) it is held outdoors, and (b) for executive jocks, it is the office Olympics— their one chance really to strut their stuff. All winter long, the lunch hours have been dominated by idle debates about whose forehand has improved the most, or who has been sandbagging his golf handicap. Now is the moment of truth.

Naturally, much office politics is mixed with sport in determining the outcome of all these office championships. It is traditional for every firm to have at least one assistant vice-president who was once a nationally ranked tennis champ; by pure chance, this is the person who annually gets teamed with the aging president in the doubles matches. For many junior execs, there is some confusion about how hard to try in these events. Win, if possible—because being company singles champion will get you lionized at the office. But at all costs don't appear overly competitive. And a word to the wise: even though it's always acceptable to beat your superiors, don't humiliate them— give them what the tennis pros call a "customer's game." If you've just taken up tennis, play with another novice on an out-of-the-way court—or sit by the pool and drink Bloody Marys.

The office outing is also the one chance you will get all year to see your associates in their civilian clothes—and out of them. Liberated from the strict codes of proper office wear, they will appear in a delightful array of outfits, ranging from Bjorn Borg pinstriped tennis jerseys to Good and Fruity–colored patchwork golf slacks. This is also the time of year when the excesses of expense-account diets are not concealed behind loose-fitting suit coats or dresses. So be sensitive to the feelings of your forty-two-year-old superiors who have developed paunches. Refrain from exhibiting skin-tight French-style swimming trunks or string bikinis, even if you've been working out all winter for just this moment.

Lesson Ten: Doing Business in the Middle East

Sooner or later in your career you will find yourself amidst the sands of Araby, trying to bring some of those petrodollars back home. It's not easy. The Saudis are different from you and me. They grew up so poor that they weren't even dirt-poor: they were sand-poor. And hot. And bored. Always a new oasis, but the same damned faces.

Then one day Abdul was shooting at some food, and up from the ground came a-bubblin' crude. Black gold. Texas tea. Saudi soda. Suddenly, they were all as rich as the forty thieves.

Those first petrodollars went to buy sunglasses, air conditioners, Datsun pickups, more camels, and maybe a few spare wives. But with all those possessions, the Saudis began to settle down and started thinking about business. After all, every rich American they knew was in business.

But what *is* business? they asked. Simple—business is what Americans do to make money and keep busy. But the Saudis didn't care about the money. They just wanted to get in on all the fun of being businessmen: having an office, a car, and a chauffeur. Getting computer printouts.

Flying Concordes to Paris for negotiations. Drinking. Throwing money at belly dancers. Keeping a mistress in London. And most of all, having those fat, sweaty American carpetbaggers kiss their feet!

And what business should we go into? they asked. Who cared—anything that would turn a profit. And what was a "profit"? Muhammad was a profit.

Thus, the cultural barriers facing an American businessman in the Middle East are formidable. The following pointers, if followed with discretion, will bring you success in your dealings with even the most byzantine oil sheik.

1. **Do** arrive several weeks late for your meeting. This will make your Saudi counterpart—who is only one week late—think you are very powerful and will show your deep understanding of Arab culture. If he is upset, glance at your watch and say, "A thousand pardons; it was Allah's will. The traffic

was heavy coming in from the airport."

2. **Do not** brush your teeth for several days before the meeting. Sit very close to your counterpart and breathe fully into his face. This is a signal in his value system that you are a personality to be reckoned with.

3. **Do** sprinkle your conversation with poetic Arabic phrases. Arabs have a weakness for their language, and by reciting a few well-practiced lines, you will be showing your appreciation for their culture. If you are not good at languages, you should at least be able to put forth your proposal in Arabic; for example, *"Turiid tashtari kam ghawasaat?"* ("Would you like to buy some nuclear submarines?")

4. **Do not** make small talk. Saudis wish to appear deep and mysterious to foreigners. They are tired of hearing Americans try to get the ball rolling with clichés like, "It's not the heat that kills you, it's the *humidity!*" Instead, sprinkle your conversation with

THE POLICY AND PROCEDURES
MANUAL

If you're the type who really needs to do things by the book, the informal rules we've compiled in this chapter may not be enough. We suggest you make your company's "policy and procedures manual" your Bible. The following is a sample page torn from one such corporate version of the Ten Commandments.

Sick Leave

The company allows all employees five days of sick leave per year, which may be accumulated over two years. Sickness as defined herein shall be an incapacitating physical illness requiring the consultation of a physician, nurse, or chiropractor requiring at least eighteen consecutive hours of bed rest. So-called mental health days taken to extend weekends, sleep off hangovers, or do errands around the house are not encouraged.

Grievances

Nobody likes a complainer, least of all the company. However, a mechanism has been created for your complaints, should you for some reason have any. First, address the problem to your immediate superior. If s/he tells you where to get off, think twice about proceeding further. Approaching your boss's boss is the next step, although this is a high-risk move. If you still do not receive satisfaction, file a formal grievance with the required signatures of your boss and boss's boss on the appropriate form, #UY-8925, available from Personnel.

Passing the Buck

The official company policy on passing the buck is not yet fully articulated. The Policy and Procedures Committee considered the issue at length before deciding to refer the matter to a firm of professional policy consultants for further deliberation.

Sexual Harassment

Employees of the company should refrain from making

phrases like "Oh, Mahmoud, my brother of brothers, I would joyfully travel a travel of fifty days to bring you this deal as fragrant as a thousand camels."

5. **Never** refuse coffee. The Bedouin host must serve you coffee to display his hospitality, and it is a serious insult to refuse. Although it has the consistency of number-four crude, smile and drink it like a Turk. Do not request Sanka.

6. **Avoid** comments such as "Your daughter is pretty," or "I think your wife is really great!" Hospitality and generosity are central to the Arab culture. Whenever a guest speaks admiringly of any of the Bedouin's possessions, it creates an obligation for the host to share them.

7. **Do not** discuss your commission in terms of "thousands" and "millions." If you say "thirty-three," without adding the word *thousand*, the sheik may write you a check for thirty-three *million* (all those zeros get confusing).

Negotiation

NEGOTIATION IS AN AN-cient business art. It traces back as far as the Book of Exodus, when the Hebrew workers who were building the Pyramids went on a wildcat strike to protest their substandard pay and unacceptable working conditions. When Moses went before Phar-oah and shouted, *"Let my people go,"* he was employ-ing a classic negotiating technique, *making the out-rageous opening demand.* When Pharaoh, in turn, re-fused to budge, he was sim-ply making the standard riposte, *calling the oppo-nent's bluff.* Finally, when Moses tired of the deadlock

and asked God to visit the ten plagues upon the Egyptians, he was resorting to the oldest gambit of all, *calling in your tough guy.*

Of course, few ordinary business confrontations are of biblical significance. But the opportunity for negotiation is part of every working day for the successful businessman or businesswoman, and there are a few standard moves that are essential to have in your repertoire.

Negotiating Thrusts and Parries

Move 1: Drawing the Bottom Line

Take the time before negotiations begin—and between negotiating sessions—to think through exactly what you *must* have in order to feel that you have not been railroaded. Know your walk-away price—the absolute bottom line you're willing to accept. Imagine that you've never made more than $18,000 in your life and find yourself

sitting across the table from a prospective boss who offers you a $40,000-a-year job—and then sweetens the pot by dangling a $5,000 cash bonus under your nose if you accept immediately. You must fight your Pavlovian response—to salivate and grab immediately for the check—and remember the $48,000 bottom line you decided on dispassionately the night before. Look your opponent in the eye, smile confidently, and say, "I'm flattered—but I turned down two offers in the sixties earlier this week."

Move 2: Sizing Up Your Opponent

Now that you've figured out what you want, put yourself in your opponent's shoes, in order to understand his strategy in approaching negotiations with *you.* Review past correspondence, letters, previous deals, and notes of meetings you have had before. Taping phone conversations for stress analysis, as well as handwriting analysis of your opponent's signature, is optional.

Move 3: The Jekyll-and-Hyde Technique

Most negotiations contain elements of both competition *and* collaboration. That's why it's always a good idea to take at least *two* negotiators to the table. Get together with your partner the night before and decide which of you feels more comfortable playing an S.O.B., and which of you would like to portray Mr. Nice Guy. This is particularly effective in drawn-out negotiations where the Nice Guy can smooth things over and keep communications open, while the S.O.B. repeatedly sneers at the other side's "best offers" by stalking away from the table, muttering that the other side is a bunch of thieves, and declaring that your side could get twice as much elsewhere. When the S.O.B. switches to offense, he presents your own team's inflated demands with the appropriate swagger. Meanwhile, the Nice Guy acts so reasonable that he often *appears* to side with your opponents.

In especially intense negotiations, the Nice Guys from both sides usually get together secretly after hours for drinks. During these informal moments, they can often come to terms that they believe can be "sold" to their respective S.O.B.'s. On cue, the S.O.B.'s suddenly moderate their demands and fade into the background while the Nice Guys sign the deal. This technique enables the Nice Guys to maximize their working relationship, while ensuring that both sides feel that they have obtained the best possible deal.

Move 4: Pretending to Leave the "Boss" at Home

A variant of the Jekyll-and-Hyde technique is to leave the S.O.B.—real or imagined—at home deliberately. After reaching the outlines of an acceptable deal, you retire from the negotiating room to a nearby office and place a call to obtain "the boss's approval." The key to this move is leaving the door ajar so that your opponents can overhear your unsuccessful attempt to sell the "boss." After a few dramatic minutes of pleading, whimpering, and begging, you return sheepishly to the table with tales of how you will be drawn and quartered unless you get several major concessions by midnight.

A common example of this technique occurs when union negotiators make a deal with management that they agree to "submit" to the rank and file for "ratification." When the rank and file reject the deal by ten to one, the union negotiator goes back to the bargaining table buoyed by a whole new set of "nonnegotiable demands" insisted on by his constituents. In merchandising this variation is known as the "Bait and Switch"; in negotiating it goes by two names: "Multiple Bites of the Apple" and "Multiple Slices of the Salami."

Lawyers also make popular absentee Hydes in this strategy, as in "I'd love to make the deal on those terms, but my lawyer would fire me."

Move 5: The Strategic Misrepresentation

It is not the place of a serious textbook to advocate the unrestricted use of lying, but it is wise to draw the distinction, as did George Washington Plunkitt, a turn-of-the-century corrupt New York politician, between the honest "strategic misrepresentation" and the "dishonest lie." What is a strategic misrepresentation? Simply put, it is tantamount to a bluff in poker: if done with finesse and in the spirit of good sportsmanship, it's all within the rules of the game.

The negotiator for the Postal Workers Union, for example, might declare that "my members are the most motivated and efficient workers in the country." *That's* a harmless strategic misrepresentation. He might continue by insisting that his rank and file would *never* accept less than a 70 percent across-the-board wage increase. He knows it's false. His opponent knows it's false. The only question is whether they will accept a 12 percent increase or hold out for 20 percent.

The dishonest lie is frowned upon, however, and its perpetrator must accept the possibility that his next move may be to a villa in Costa Rica or a small room in Allenwood. The dishonest lie is something truly misleading or even fraudulent. Examples include falsification of accounting documents, forgery, and selling property you don't own. This is not acceptable behavior, although it is wise to be aware of these sorts of curve balls, lest an over-zealous opponent try to bean you with one.

Move 6: Choosing Sites

In most competitive sports, it is always better to have the home court advantage. This is generally true in competitive negotiation as well. As host you gain invaluable control over setting the agenda, deciding on seating arrangements, and other small factors that can put psychological pressure on the other side. Or you can increase the deadline pressure by taking your opponents on a full day's tour of your "beautiful" city, refusing to get down to business until just a few hours before their plane is ready to leave.

Occasionally, however, you may want to do your bargaining on a neutral site. Or you may want to meet at your opponents' offices if you feel you have something to hide—like the fact that your office furniture was repossessed last week.

THE "STRATEGIC MISREPRESENTATION": HOW TO SUCCEED IN BUSINESS WITHOUT REALLY LYING

There are many times in the corporate environment when it is inconvenient—or even suicidal—to tell the truth. But no moral businessman will ever consciously lie. Here is a list of the dozen most common "strategic misrepresentations" used in business.

1. "Your check is in the mail."

2. "The customer is always right."

3. "Let's get together for lunch sometime."

4. "There's no such thing as a free lunch."

5. "It's not the lousy hundred grand that counts—it's the principle of the thing."

6. "This special sixteen-piece set is not available in any store."

7. "I'm from corporate headquarters and I'm here to help."

8. "This company is run in the interests of the shareholders."

9. "The numbers tell the whole story."

10. "Look . . . I know this really honest accountant (lawyer, broker, developer)."

11. "That's absolutely my rock bottom offer."

12. "Trust me."

Other Hints

• When in doubt, say "no." It's always easier to reverse an initial "no" than an initial "yes."

• Be well rested and well fed. Avoid drinking too much coffee so that if negotiations drag on, you can win the Battle of the Bladder.

• Avoid polarizing phrases (unless you are playing the role of S.O.B.) like *rip-off* or *obscene profit*.

• Throw enough absurd throwaway issues into your initial demands so that you can appear to be making generous concessions without giving anything substantive away.

• If your eyes give you away when the going gets tough, wear sunglasses.

5

CAREER
MANAGEMENT

A Career
Playbook

IN THE WORLD OF SPORT, it is possible for a first-year recruit to become the most valuable player from the moment he walks onto the field. In his rookie year, Kareem Abdul Jabbar brought an also-ran basketball team, the Milwaukee Bucks, from the bottom of the league to the NBA championship. In his rookie year, Earl Campbell became such a powerful runner for the Houston Oilers that his coach built the entire offense around him.

But rookie years in the business world are different. They may ask you to suit up in full pads before coming to the office every day; they may put you through exercise drills and quiz you on your grasp of strategy and tactics—but don't count on carrying the ball in a big game for a long time. During these early stages, you might as well accept your status on the second string. There's only one thing to do to become a starter: keep your head down, listen up during huddles—and hustle every time you take the field.

But when the day comes that the coach finally taps *you* as quarterback, you'd better have a game plan and a repertoire of plays appropriate for every situation. For those of you who are unfamiliar with calling your own game, we have put together a career playbook that includes a few of the most popular and successful plays.

PLAY ONE: GROUND YARDAGE

Slow going, but steady progress. This low-risk strategy is advisable for the first several downs after the start of your career; it is the most common way to gain yardage in large corporations and professional firms. Most young players must spend many seasons blocking for others before getting a chance to carry the ball themselves. Can produce a touchdown, but only after a long, unbroken drive.

Play One: GROUND YARDAGE

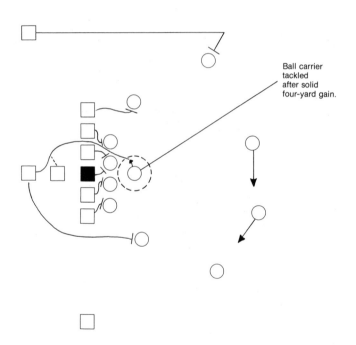

Ball carrier
tackled
after solid
four-yard gain.

PLAY TWO: THE LATERAL

You've been stuck in the same no-glory position for the past five years, and you can't seem to find any holes in the defense. It's obvious that with your current qualifications your career path is stymied: to advance forward, you first have to make a quick cut to the sidelines. If it's early in your career, take time out and get your "union card," an M.B.A., J.D., or C.P.A. If you are a mid-career corporate bureaucrat, take a job in the federal government for two or three years. For some totally mysterious reason, a little experience at the biggest and least efficient bureaucracy of all qualifies an executive for a corporate job three levels higher than the one he left.

Play Two: THE LATERAL

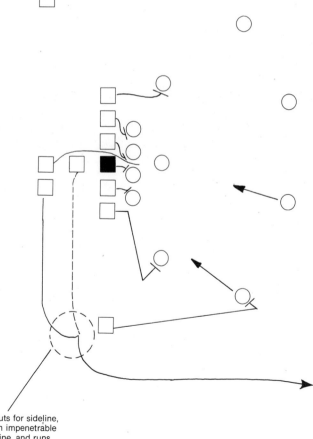

Receiver cuts for sideline,
avoiding an impenetrable
defensive line, and runs
for the open field.

PLAY THREE: THE LONG BOMB

For those who would rather be a spectacular failure than a dismal success. No longer satisfied with two- or three-yard gains, you break away from the pack, run a zig-out pattern, and go for the big score. Gene Amdahl executed a perfect long bomb when he left his job as head of R & D at IBM to form his own large-scale computer company. He's now worth tens of millions.

But the long bomb is not for everybody: for every high-scoring receiver who winds up on the cover of a national magazine, there are a hundred who drop the ball in front of everybody. Still, for would-be entrepreneurs, it's better to try and fail than to spend the rest of your life complaining that you could have caught the ball too, if you'd only bothered to go long.

Play Three: THE LONG BOMB

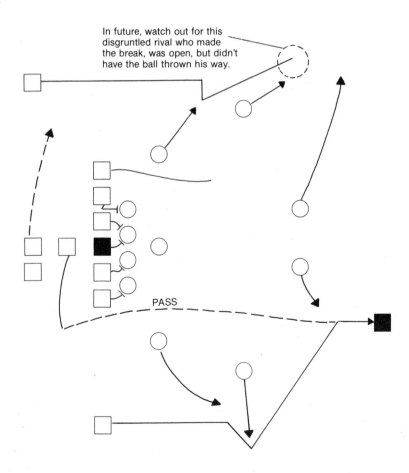

In future, watch out for this disgruntled rival who made the break, was open, but didn't have the ball thrown his way.

PASS

PLAY FOUR: THE BOOTLEG

The quarterback, tired of fighting with an uncreative coach or parsimonious owner, decides he'd rather jump leagues than play with his old team any longer. He takes the snap—and to everyone's surprise, including his own team's, keeps the ball and runs with it himself . . . to another shop. The bootleg is especially common in the oil industry, where geologists constantly switch jerseys looking for the big score.

Note: The quarterback, running in the open field without blockers, risks being blind-sided by a blitzing safety who has read the play in advance. The role of safety is usually played by the company's legal department, which has previously gotten the quarterback to agree in writing that he will *not* switch to a competing team.

Play Four: THE BOOTLEG

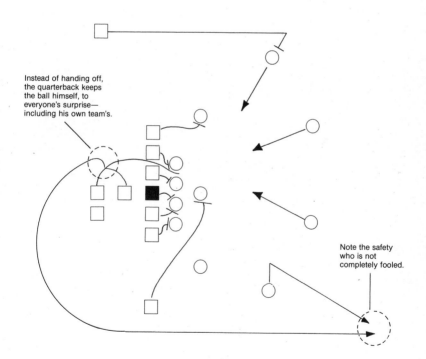

Instead of handing off, the quarterback keeps the ball himself, to everyone's surprise—including his own team's.

Note the safety who is not completely fooled.

PLAY FIVE: THE PUNT

You're in over your head in a new job, or your division's gone sour and is losing yardage fiendishly. In these situations discretion is often the better part of valor. It's time to divest yourself of the ball and let someone else carry it before you're thrown for a safety.

Top executives who resort to this play ask a headhunter to line up a new job for them—usually with a bigger title and higher pay. Then they exit quietly, leaving an unsuspecting junior executive holding the bag when the flop hits the fan. The punt is also popular among entrepreneurs who see that their hot young growth companies are in for deep water ahead. They sell out to a gullible conglomerate and retire to Florida with the proceeds.

Play Five: THE PUNT

Note punter's footsteps leading
directly to the bench even before
the play is completely over.

PLAY SIX: THE SACK

A quarterback's nightmare. The quarterback's own team, tired of his exorbitant salary, glory grabbing, and miserable play calling, decides to take him out of the game before he has a chance to lose the team any more big yardage. A recent example of the sack was the forced resignation of Fred Silverman from the presidency of NBC when the network was still languishing at number three in the ratings . . . two full years after Silverman publicly promised to turn things around.

To avoid the sack, be nice to your colleagues on the way up the ladder: you never know whom you'll meet on the way down. And never promise more than you can deliver.

Play Six: THE SACK

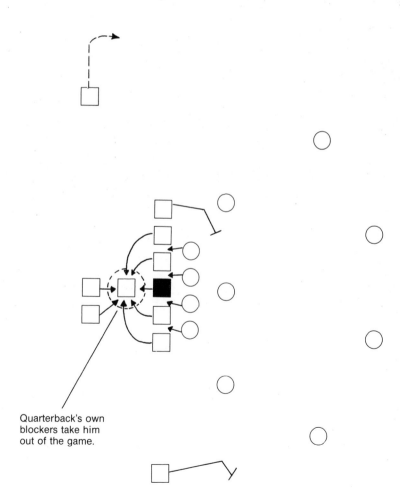

Quarterback's own
blockers take him
out of the game.

BEING STALKED
BY A
HEADHUNTER

After expanding your résumé and interviewing for scores of jobs, you finally pick a company and dig in at work. But the process of recruiting doesn't end there: all the companies that turned you down a year ago for the Catch-22 of lacking experience consider you a prime candidate—now that somebody else has picked up the cost of your training (and your first expensive mistakes).

The essential difference between recruiting at school and recruiting in the executive "aftermarket" is that employers no longer approach you directly. Instead, you enter the free agent draft, courtesy of an executive search firm (or, more commonly, "headhunter").

Headhunting is tricky business. Potential candidates must be approached in a way that does not tip off their current employer. Consequently, headhunters usually identify themselves with a phony name and firm to get past your secretary. Once *you* are on the line, however, the headhunter will reveal his true identity and pop the big question: for a few extra thousand and a bigger office, are you willing to walk?

Usually, the headhunter knows enough about you to bait the hook expertly. Don't ask how, but somehow he or she has been given your name, phone number, and an old résumé. You become intrigued by his glowing description of the possible job opportunity. You set up a series of mail drops and agree on places to deposit microdots of your new résumé. The plot thickens.

Thus begins a series of clandestine telephone calls between you and the headhunter. Each time the recruiter calls your office he will give a different name and company, in order to deceive the receptionist. One headhunter we know uses the presidential series, announcing himself as Mr. Washington on the first call, Mr. Adams on the next, and so on.

But don't get carried away. Remember that these corporate body snatchers work for some company, not for you. Just as you expanded your résumé, headhunters are wont to hail every position from manager of accounts payable on up as "exciting," with "high visibility," "a unique opportunity."

If you should find yourself

seeking to make the big switch, but haven't yet been contacted by headhunters, we suggest asking a close friend at another company to have his headhunter try to recruit you. Of course, you refuse the job offer in this instance, but get your foot in the door with the headhunting firm, who will keep your résumé on active file for life.

"Great news! I've located a complete idiot."

Time Management

TIME IS MONEY—AND IF there's one thing a business person can't afford to waste, it's money. As a result, there are any number of books available on how to manage your time. Most are two or three hundred pages long and are filled with perennial time-saving tips like sleep less, delegate more, and put a telephone in your car. And most are themselves a total waste of time. As any time-management book will tell you, an executive's day is too precious to waste reading anything but condensations, journal articles, and the newspaper. Herein is a mercifully brief distillation of the essentials of time management.

To get a rough idea of how much time you cur-

rently waste, all you have to do is keep an accurate diary of exactly how you spend each minute of your average business day. Unless you are extremely efficient, the odds are your time-efficiency analysis will look fairly similar to the one our researchers recently recorded at a major corporation:

Activity	Time used
Getting coffee	31 min.
Reading newspaper (horoscope, used car and help wanted ads)	42 min.
Playing telephone tag	29 min.
Flirting with secretary	10 min.
Productive morning work	63 min.
Completing time sheets for control department	27 min.
Complying with excessive federal regulations	1 hr., 18 min.
Lunch	1 hr., 52 min.
Tabulating department's winnings on office pro football pool	33 min.
Talking with spouse about weekend plans	21 min.
Camping out in somebody else's reception area	18 min.
Productive afternoon work	84 min.
Telling jokes to clients	10 min.
Listening to clients' jokes	11 min.
Shepherding reports through word processing	41 min.
TOTAL TIME BILLABLE TO CLIENTS	9 hr., 47 min.

To get into the habit of using your time efficiently, you must become your own taskmaster. First you have to decide what you wish to accomplish in your business career and in your personal life—if you have one. But it's not as easy as just drawing up a wish list: making a few million, playing the *Emperor* Concerto in Carnegie Hall, staying in shape, raising a happy family. A successful business career consists of a series of trade-offs: you must learn to focus on certain objectives to the temporary exclusion of others. You must learn to do what *has* to be done and *stonewall* on everything else, depending on your priorities: if you have a family, you don't want to get stuck on business in Peoria during Billy's first birthday.

Deciding what your priorities are requires developing what is known as a *life strategy*. Many time-management authors suggest the "Armageddon approach" to developing such a priority list, wherein you list your top twenty life objectives on a piece of paper and ask yourself which you would choose to accomplish if you could complete only five before the world came to an end. This approach is dangerous, however, because the instinct of many short-term optimizers is to make two weeks at Club Med their first choice.

Instead, we suggest the far more reliable *peer pressure approach:* imagine you are writing your own obituary for your college alumni magazine, and ask yourself what life accomplishments you would like to be able to include. Of course, try to be realistic about these goals, or someone else may be writing your obituary sooner than you think.

Time-Management Tactics

Armed with your new life strategy, you can now move to the tactical level of day-to-day implementation. It's not enough to try the obvious techniques of making your memos *short*, dictating everything, and acting on each incoming piece of correspondence only once, so that you don't have to read it again a month later before making the decision. Successful business people are obsessive list makers; we suggest that you become one, too.

Every morning, make a list of all the tasks you must accomplish during the day; then label them "Urgent," "Important but Not Urgent," and "Mañana." **Urgent** items might include "File required 10-K forms with SEC regarding new stock offering before midnight deadline" and "Get shirts laundered." **Important but Not Urgent** items might include "Attend Christmas party task force meeting" and "Requisition new brass nameplate for office door." **Mañana** is reserved for items like "Read trade journals *(Modern Plastics, Chicken World)* and "Balance personal checkbook."

Your Own Personal Billing Rate

An even better way of allocating your time requires first estimating how many dollars per hour you think your time is really worth. Only then can you best select those activities that will maximize your economic gain. We are acquainted with a chief executive making a seven-figure salary who will go an hour out of his way to buy a record on sale. To save 98 cents he wastes $500 worth of his time.

As you move up the corporate hierarchy, your implicit billing rate will rise. The following is an estimate of the rational shifts in your life-style that should accompany each increase in your personal billing rate.

Position	Billing rate	Life-style
Mail clerk	Minimum wage	• Take bus to work • Cut out 10-cents-off coupons from office magazines before distributing them. • Travel across town to borrow books from the library. • Brown-bag lunch. • Get high at break. • Sit in bleachers at ball game.
Sales trainee	$10/hour	• Commute in time-financed Datsun 280-ZX. • Ignore bargains except when buying cases of Heineken. • Purchase paperbacks. • Send laundry to dry cleaner. • Eat at company cafeteria.

		• Sit in reserved seats at ball game.
Junior executive	**$20/hour**	• Travel by plane on all trips of more than 100 miles.
		• Shop for bargains only on big-ticket items like TVs, cars, and houses.
		• Purchase hardcovers.
		• Hire weekly maid service for apartment.
		• Eat lunch at nearby restaurant.
		• Watch ball game on midnight videotape delay.
Senior executive	**$50/hour**	• Travel first class so that you can board and deplane rapidly.
		• Don't worry about bargains. Ask your secretary to do your shopping for you.
		• Hire full-time housekeeper.
		• Eat at corporate dining room.
		• Sit in corporate box for major sports events.
Chief executive	**$100/hour**	• Fly via corporate jet.
		• Hire a secretary for your secretary.
		• Spend at least 59 percent of your time figuring out how to avoid confiscatory taxes, since the government is taking at least 60 percent of your income.
		• Brown-bag your lunch; your time is too valuable to waste on formal meals.
		• Buy pro sports franchise and sit in dugout with players.

What to Do When There's Nothing to Do

The corporate life usually demands a furious pace. Nevertheless, most executives have to suffer through occasional odd days, weeks, even months when there's absolutely nothing to do. Perhaps you're between assignments, you can't make a move until interest rates drop, or it's the Friday before Labor Day and you're the only one left holding down the fort. These occasions may sound like welcome respites, but if you're still stuck in the bullpen, or work in a fish-bowl office with glass doors, it can be excruciating to be idle in full public view. Busyness in business is critical: *looking* as if you have your finger in the dike at all times is one of the most oft-neglected aspects of time management.

Whether you have this problem only once in a while or are in a job that is totally expendable, here's a guide to the preferred techniques of looking gainfully employed when there's nothing to do.

1. Newspapers are always a good bet. But keep your calculator turned on, a yellow pad and pencil handy, and your finger poised for a quick flip to the stock quotations. That way, if you hear heavy footsteps while you're sneaking a look at Ann Landers, it will look as if you're performing complicated ratio analysis.

2. Alternatively, pick up the telephone and jawbone a customer or supplier. It doesn't matter who, but sound authoritative. If no one is available, all is not lost: call up the weather, Dial-a-Prayer, or the time. Take notes, and nod your head furiously while muttering, "Thanks, Frank, that's beautiful" or "Okay, but remember you owe me one!"

3. Hide out in an executive washroom stall and finish the new James Clavell novel.

4. Go to the supply closet and search compulsively for the right color felt-tip.

5. Reorganize your files.

6. Insert crumpled paper into the copying machine paper tray and push the start button. Then spend half an hour trying to unjam it.

7. Rush back and forth between the water cooler, the office cafeteria, the copying machine, the scheduling board, and your work area, carrying an armload of computer printouts.

8. Update your résumé.

Apply these eight suggestions religiously, and your reputation for unfailing industriousness will soon earn you a private office. Pretty soon everybody —even your superiors— will have to make an appointment to see you. By then, behind the security perimeter of an outer office, a closed door, and a loyal secretary, you're home free.

Women in Business

INCREASINGLY, THE MA-jor decision makers in corporate America are as likely to be wearing perfume as after-shave. This is not to say that women haven't been calling the shots in business for a long time. For decades it has been the role of the secretary to *manage* her boss, making sure she presented his best face to the world and covered up his rough edges and flaws.

But it has been only within recent memory that women have begun to receive their fair share of formal recognition, rank, and salary. Doors to the executive suite are now opening to women in increasing numbers (although most women are still denied access to those two special rooms where male executives can do their business in a relaxed atmosphere: the locker room and the washroom).

The traditional businesswoman's attire: *attractive suit, reasonable shoes. A bow at the neck is optional (and unfathomable to the men in your office), but goes a long way to differentiate you from the secretarial pool.*

Barriers to Entry

Most *formal* barriers to the entry of women into business have been eliminated, but many *cultural* ones remain. When businessmen relax, they generally head for the nearest bar and talk about sports, women, and money —not necessarily in that order. They generally enjoy it when a woman colleague joins them, but often become edgy if she tries to balance the conversation with talk of ballet, the ERA, or Mary Cunningham.

It's not that women can *never* be fully accepted in these activities; but what mature woman in her right mind would ever want to? Who *cares* that Green Bay is favored to beat the Rams by five and a half? Who would ever *want* to kill a perfectly good Monday night listening to Frank Gifford get into a heavy rap with Howard Cosell?

But there are times when being able to bluff a passing interest in major-league sports can be of great importance to a woman on the move. For those who feel uncertain of the difference between a touchdown and a touchback, we present the following compendium to help you talk a good game, beginning with the fall season.

1. Football: Eleven men on each side knock each other senseless trying to move the ball an average of three yards per play. Only

One of the boys: *hair pulled back, horn-rimmed glasses, a scowl. Ready to cuss, drink, talk sports, and infight with the best of 'em. Wear this look and the threatened top executives in your office will run for cover.*

professional football is important, played by teams like the Dallas Cowboys, the Los Angeles Rams, and the Ohio State Buckeyes. Important players to know: Terry Bradshaw, Herschel Walker, Bubba Smith, and Whizzer White. NFL commissioner: Pistol Pete Rozelle. As in all sports, if the local team is a loser, you don't even have to take the time to follow them. When the boys in the office start talking about last night's game, you can always land on your feet by complaining: "Don't talk to me about the New England Patriots [Cleveland Browns, Green Bay Packers, et al.]. After those clowns choked last year, I gave up for good."

2. Basketball: Five seven-footers per side jump into the air every twenty-four seconds. AKA "roundball," "B-ball," or (to romanticizing sportswriters) "the city game." Important players to know: Julius Erving (Dr. J), Larry Bird (the Great White Hope), Marvin "Magic" Johnson, and Kareem Abdul Jabbar (formerly Lew Alcindor).

NBA commissioner: Larry O'Brien. Standard complaint to use in the office elevator: "The NBA bores me until the playoffs." Alternatively: "I'm tired of having the Warriors [the Celtics, the 76ers, etc.] win the game, only to have it taken away by the refs!"

3. Baseball: Nine players per side chew tobacco and look bored and rather unathletic for three hours, while pitcher and catcher play keep-away with the batter. Key players: Reggie Jackson, Steve Garvey, Joe DiMaggio, Marvin Miller. Baseball commissioner: Bowie Kuhn, an ex-lawyer who watches the World Series every year in his shirt-sleeves just to prove that it's all right to play October night games in thirty-degree weather. Classic phrases to use in the office: "I hate the Yankees—they're just a money team. Dave Winfield makes more than the president of Exxon." Better yet: "Of course Brett [or any other current player] is great, but no one will ever compare with Ted Williams."

Dealing with Male Chauvinists

Admittedly, it is annoying to be constantly treated to lunches and dinners and to have others carry your heavy luggage on business trips or open doors for you. But it's important to keep your sense of humor around the office, no matter how sorely

tested. If at an important conference your boss asks you to get the coffee, spare him a blistering barrage of feminist invective. Like most executives who cut their professional teeth thirty years ago, the man probably just needs a refresher course.

The first step in reprogramming these fossils is to post the following guide to sexist language promi-

TAKING THE "MAN" OUT OF "MANAGEMENT": A GUIDE TO SEXIST LANGUAGE

Old Phrase	Current Accepted Version
Chairman	Chairperson
Salesman	Salesperson
Manhattan	Personhattan
He	S/he or he/she
She's got great legs	S/he's got great legs
Man hour	Work hour
Sexy	Attractive
Miss, Mrs., or "Cynthia"	Ms.
Get into bed with XYZ Corp.	Establish a meaningful relationship with XYZ Corp.
Monthlies	30-day sales reports
Girl, broad	Woman, female
Dicker	Negotiate
Bitchy	Assertive
Secretary	Administrative assistant
Balls	Balls

nently throughout the office. Everyone will appreciate the tip.

Office Romance

In recent years, as women have entered business in greater numbers, the press has made much over the possibilities for women to "advance through romance." Avoid this strategy like the plague. Office romance rumors cast a long shadow over the real reason for a woman's success in business. (The only exception to this is for women who are presidents of their own companies: as Andy Warhol once observed, your own employees make great dates because "you don't have to pick them up and they're always tax-deductible.")

Keeping the Office Wolf from Your Door

To make it clear that you're not available, we suggest displaying a photograph of your husband, boyfriend, or significant other(s) prominently on your desk and occasionally dropping references to the

Loaded for bear: skin-tight pants, ruffled hair, a smoldering look in the eye. Wears Tabu. This is how your male co-workers envision you in their wildest fantasies, but it's difficult for them to take you seriously when they have trouble keeping their eyes on your proformas. Use only with extreme caution.

fact that you played tennis all weekend with "Jack." When dining alone on a business trip, bring your briefcase to the table and pretend to be going through papers from time to time.

Of course, these gambits may not always deter the pinstriped Don Juans who think the best way of paying a woman a compliment is to make a pass at her. If giving him a rain check for when the Dow hits 2,000 doesn't work, casually inform him that the office secretarial pool gave him only a "4." If *that* doesn't give him the hint, call the company's sexual harassment coordinator and "cry wolf."

Assertiveness Training

Being sweet and agreeable is a laudable quality, but recent studies show that many women feel uncomfortable being aggressive around men. This is a problem (see *The Managerial Woman* by Hennig and Jardin). To succeed in business, you must occasionally project an image of toughness, lest the aggressive businessmen you encounter turn your career into a replay of "Bambi Meets Godzilla." We have developed the following true-to-life *assertiveness training* exercises to help you improve your ability to stick up for yourself.

A NINE-WEEK ASSERTIVENESS TRAINING COURSE

WEEK NUMBER	ACTIVITY
1	Pose, hands on hips, in front of a mirror for fifteen minutes nightly, repeating "no" forcefully.
2	Buy a copy of Helen Reddy's "I Am Woman" and memorize the lyrics. Practice singing it first thing every morning with three or four other women from your office.
3	Dispute your car repair bill . . . for a change.
4	Pit your driving skills against those of cab drivers during rush hour (Week 7 in New York).
5	Buy one share of Dow Chemical stock and interrupt the chairman during the annual meeting with a barbed question on the company's affirmative action policies.
6	Order Château Lafitte at the fanciest restaurant in town. Then send it back after tasting, telling the sommelier, "I asked for *wine*—not Welch's."
7	Point to a "No Smoking" sign and demand that the six-foot-three piece of beef next to you put out his cigar.
8	Dial information and demand unlisted phone numbers.
9	Follow a hard-to-get male colleague into the men's room for a conference by the head.

6

HOW TO KEEP SCORE

or

"I founded my own $10 million company, but my ex-roommate's the executive V.P. of Exxon. Am I ahead?"

ONEY AND POWER are undeniably important, but it is the naive M.B.A. who thinks they are everything. Back in the 1960s, social psychologists who studied the personal expectations of our affluent society formulated a concept they called the "hierarchy of needs." The idea was that the first things a person wanted were food and shelter, while things like cars and food processors became absolute necessities only after the more basic wants were satisfied. A few years later, professors of organizational behavior repackaged the hierarchy concept for the business world. Begin at the bottom of the following chart and read upward through the three categories:

1. Things an executive needs for survival.

2. Things an executive needs to achieve self-respect.

3. Things an executive needs for "self-actualization" (O.B. lingo for a "natural high").

EXECUTIVE HIERARCHY OF PERKS*

Self-actualization

A secretary still willing to make coffee
Appearance on the cover of *Fortune*
Company jet
Appointment to a presidential commission
Corner office with two windows
Keys to the executive washroom

Respect

A reserved parking space
An office with a door
A pretentious title
A personal secretary
Stock options

Survival

Company car
Dental & health coverage
A safe workplace
Two weeks' vacation
A job . . . any job

*with apologies to Abraham Maslow's hierarchy of needs

BEGIN HERE

Got the idea? Below, we provide a questionnaire to help you evaluate your achievements and gauge your true business status. If you finish with **1,000 points or more,** you've already made it and should seriously consider retiring from business in favor of something more aesthetically rewarding, such as retiring to Tahiti to paint the natives in romantic settings. If you score **250 to 999,** have a cardiologist examine your heart *immedi-* *ately*—you're almost at the pinnacle, but the sheer ecstasy of getting there can be extremely hazardous (our medical consultants recommend twenty milligrams of Valium every six hours).

If you score **less than 250,** don't worry—you ought to have plenty of spare time to work on your tennis game. And if you're **disqualified,** buy a set of colored pencils and reread this book *very* carefully before taking the test again.

How to Keep Score: A Career Evaluation Quiz

	Points
LOCATION AND TYPE OF EMPLOYMENT	
Work at local sales office	3
Work at regional headquarters	6
Work at corporate headquarters	11
Work for yourself	
At office	21
At home	5
Out of your car	Automatic disqualification

YOUR WORK AREA—physical layout

Office with door	2
Window office	5
Corner office	10
View of parking lot or air shaft	−3
View of harbor, river, or skyline	8
Private reception area	12
Office with private bath	27
Office shared with more than two others	−1
A cubicle in the bullpen	Automatic disqualification

YOUR OFFICE—furnishings

Wall-to-wall carpeting	1
Oriental rug	9
Linoleum	−3
Metal venetian blinds	−5
Plastic plants	−12
Couch and coffee table	11
Couch with sofabed	16
Antique grandfather clock	40
Original Picasso	105
Leroy Nieman prints	Automatic disqualification

OFFICE TELECOMMUNICATIONS

Basic black office phone	1
Phone with multiple lines and HOLD button	3
Speaker phone	7
Muzak during "hold"	−20
Electronic office system with call forwarding, conference calls, etc.	8
WATS line, 800 number	14
Private line that circumvents switchboard	27
Pay phone only	Automatic disqualification

YOUR SECRETARIES AND ASSISTANTS

Office temp only	0
One secretary	2

Two secretaries	5
Three or more secretaries	25
Unemployed model who can't type as secretary (if male executive)	21
Male secretary (if woman executive)	35
Recent M.B.A. as executive assistant	29
Personal bodyguards	51
Secretarial pool only	Automatic disqualification

YOUR SALARY—mode and frequency of payment

Weekly check	1
Biweekly check	3
Monthly check	11
Annual stock options or profit-sharing	34
Cash by the hour	Automatic disqualification

YOUR SALARY—amount

Making your age (for example, at least $25,000 for a twenty-five-year-old executive)	6
Making your height (in inches)	12
Making your weight	81
Making your shoe size	Automatic disqualification

YOUR CAR—make, model, and mileage

A car	4
J-car, K-car, X-car	10
Z-car	15
Honda, VW, Toyota (if in Northeast or California)	12
Honda, VW, Toyota (if in the South, Texas, or Detroit)	−38
Mercedes	19
Production-line Cadillac	½
Cadillac stretch limo with phone, bar, Kevlar bulletproofing, and chauffeur trained in counterterrorist driving techniques	85
Pre-1978 gas guzzler	−5
Post-1978 gas guzzler	Automatic disqualification

"First it's sex, then money; then you weed out, simplify, and you find power is enough."

BUSINESS TRAVEL

Tourist class	4
First class	9
Concorde	22
Corporate jet	49
with helicopter	101
Private rail car	74
Any mode of travel requiring exact change	Automatic disqualification

HOME ENTERTAINMENT SYSTEMS

Color TV	2
Panasonic or RCA six-foot video screen	26

No TV (on principle)	41
Roof antenna	1
Cable with Home Box Office	4
Twelve-foot dish antenna (for direct satellite reception)	93
Home video recorder	15
Videodisks	14
Home Space Invaders or Asteroids system	− 17
Black and white only	Automatic disqualification

YOUR HOME—recreational facilities

Exercycle or treadmill	1
Weights	3
Nautilus machine	12
Swimming pool	26
Tennis court	26
Both	91
Ping-Pong table in basement	6
Pool table in basement	11
Billiards table in billiards room	36
Magic Fingers vibrating bed	Automatic disqualification

BIGGEST MEDIA APPEARANCE

Brief squib in *Fortune, Business Week,* or *Forbes*	30
Profile in *People*	61
Named *Time*'s "Man of the Year"	216
Photographed with U.S. President	54
Photographed with Jack Nicklaus	72
Write-up in company newsletter for giving blood	− 8
Grilled by Mike Wallace on *60 Minutes*	Automatic disqualification

HIGHEST BUSINESS HONOR OR AWARD

Asked to join local Rotary Club	8
Elected president of national trade association	36

Nominated Secretary of Treasury	163
Have street named in your honor in hometown	25
Tapped for membership in Bohemian Club	74
Given honorary Ph.D. by college that flunked you thirty years before	59
Written up in *Who's Who*	23
Biography listed in *Cyclopedia of Young Superachievers,* Volume XLI, for payment of $125 (an extra $85 for inclusion of picture)	Automatic disqualification

TAX STATUS

File 1040A (short form)	1
File 1040 (long form) with help of H & R Block	4
Itemize deductions	9
Income averaging	23
Set up Clifford trusts for children with help of Price Waterhouse	41
Pay more to tax lawyers and accountants than you would have paid to the IRS	Automatic disqualification

YOUR PERSONAL INVESTMENTS

$10,000 in money market fund	8
Gold in Swiss vault	14
Loan to brother-in-law	− 12
Collectibles:	
Original lithographs	23
Claes Oldenburg soft sculpture	132
Raku pottery	41
$10,000 in U.S. Savings Bonds	− 25
Limited partnership in 12:1 tax shelter disallowed by IRS	Automatic disqualification

7

BUZZWORD GLOSSARY

**Cannibalization versus
Missionary Selling**

I N *My Fair Lady*, Professor Henry Higgins cons London society into accepting a common flower girl as an elegant lady by teaching her a few polite phrases. Similarly, the M.B.A., by careful study over two grueling years, can palm himself off as the Pygmalion of the boardroom by developing a devastating facility with the business terminology known as "buzzwords."

Spend a few weeks memorizing all of the following terms and shorthand abbreviations. Then practice with your friends so that you can slip them naturally into conversation. When you can achieve a rate of five B.P.M. (buzzwords per minute), you will be ready to talk your way into a high-visibility job at just about any company in corporate America.

AA The second-highest bond rating issued by Moody's and Standard & Poor's rating services. Also refers to an organization that retreads bottle-fatigued executives.

Battle of the Bladder An extremely risky negotiating technique calling for long hours, many cups of coffee, and extreme willpower and endurance.

Bells and Whistles The sexy features used to sweeten unattractive financial instruments or deals, such as call options, warrants, convertibility into common stock, or pinup-quality stock certificates (see illustration).

Beta A measure of the systematic risk inherent in a portfolio of stocks. Trotted out by M.B.A.'s to describe the risk of almost anything from commodities to personal relationships, as in "Lynn, you're a tiger, but I need more stability in life. Your beta is a little too high."

Business Ethics 1. The code of conduct observed by most responsible business executives. 2. To nearsighted business critics, an oxymoron similar to "military intelligence" and "American culture."

Cannibalization A marketing term describing increased sales of a new product that are gained by cutting the heart out of the sales of an old product (see *Missionary Selling*).

Cash Flow 1. The amount of cash earned ("thrown off") by a business, calculated by adding depreciation and deferred taxes to reported earnings. 2. A term used by executives to describe their personal financial situations, as in "Could you float me twenty bucks? The automatic teller machine was down this morning, so I'm a little short on the cash flow."

C.E.O. "Chief executive officer"—the top dog.

C.I.A. "Cash in advance."

C.O.P. "Corridors of power."

Corporate Vietnam A devastating phrase used to put down another executive's pet proposal, as in "Go head to head against Grecian Formula 16 in the male hair-coloring market? Are you trying to get us into another Corporate Vietnam?"

Counterintuitive Unclear, not believable, false. A word reserved for certain conversations with your boss, as in "Yes, I completely agree with your conclusions—as counterintuitive as they might seem."

C.P.A. "Certified public accountant." Also stands for "constant pain in the ass." A bean counter.

C.Y.A. A military term, as in "Cover your rear." The overriding decision rule used in most corporate decision making.

D & B Dun & Bradstreet. A service that performs credit checks on other companies.

D.M.U. "Decision-making unit."

Driven Another A.P.B. (all-purpose buzzword) used as a suffix to describe what makes a particular business or industry tick; thus, production-driven, marketing-driven, technology-driven, personnel-driven, etc. Also used to describe the character of certain executives.

Dumping Undercutting foreign competition by selling goods in *their* country at a price less than you charge at home in Japan. Examples of U.S. indus-

tries that are being dumped on these days: steel, autos, textiles, TVs.

Dynamic An all-purpose hype adjective. Used by headhunters to describe any unfilled job position or any burned-out executive they are trying to place. Also used as a noun by securities salesmen in lieu of words their customers might actually understand, as in "It is our opinion that the distributed computer dynamic is *the* single most important trend in technology . . . Paradyne's products all participate, one way or another, in this major technology dynamic."

E.D.P. "Electronic data processing." For noncomputer-oriented executives, synonymous with I.B.M.

E.P.S. "Earnings per share." The primitive yardstick used by most stockholders to evaluate a company's performance. Also used by primitive corporate boards to evaluate the chief executive's per-

DUNGEONS AND DRAGONS: A CORPORATE FAIRY TALE

THE CHARACTERS:

Sleeping Beauty: a profitable company whose stock is undervalued and furnishes a prime target for a takeover by another company.

Damsel in Distress: a money-losing corporation well endowed with enormous tax-loss carryforwards—which are attractive to acquiring companies that can take advantage of them.

Pirate: a raiding company trying to take over another company at the point of a sword.

Fairy Godmothers: the investment bankers who advise Damsels, Beauties, and Pirates, collecting a large share of the kingdom as a reward.

White Knight: a gallant, wealthy nobleman called in by a Sleeping Beauty's Godmother to save her from being taken by a Pirate.

Dungeon: the bullpen in an investment bank where young associates languish one hundred hours a week.

Dragon: a fire-breathing antitrust lawyer from the Justice Department.

THE STORY:

Once upon a time in a faraway land there lived a Sleeping Beauty named Conoco—a maiden so lovely that none who beheld her charms could resist them. Then one day a Pirate ship appeared on the horizon, flying the flag of Four Roses and threatening to take Conoco away and pillage her.

That night, as Conoco wept at the thought of her fate, a Fairy Godmother she had on retainer appeared, promising to search the kingdom far and wide for a White Knight to save her. The next day the White Knight arrived, his armor gleaming with Teflon, his horse laden with jewels, stock, and debentures. The Pirate ship sailed away, lowering its flag, and Conoco and the White Knight lived happily ever after.

formance—and set his bonus. Consequently, many top managers devote more time to *managing* E.P.S. than they do to managing the company.
Fast Track B.A., M.B.A., C.E.O., . . . D.O.A.

FIFO/LIFO "First in, first out," and "last in, first out." Two different methods of accounting for inventory and the cost of goods a company sells. FIFO assumes that the oldest goods in inventory are sold first; LIFO assumes that they're sold last. During periods of high inflation, choice of either the FIFO or LIFO method of accounting can have an enormous effect on the profitability of a corporation, because new inventory always costs more than old inventory. A crowded subway car uses LIFO in moving passengers in and out, whereas a crowded restaurant uses FIFO.

Go-Go Years The period from 1966 to 1969, when the stock market was flying and superheated issues like Equity Funding and National Student Marketing sold for a hundred times earnings. Not to be confused with the No-Go Years (1969–1982).

Goodwill A company's intangible assets, such as its brand name, reputation, or dealer network, which are thought to improve earning power. For example, the brand name Coca-Cola enjoys enormous goodwill worldwide, whereas the brand name DC-10 does not.

Hidden Agenda A person's *secret* motivations. For example, if a bureaucrat negotiating a juicy government contract is dickering too much over insignificant contract terms, his or her hidden agenda may be to stall until you agree to reconvene negotiations in a more congenial spot like Atlantic City or Vegas.

Indexation Varying with inflation. The prices of many goods and services, such as wages or Social Security, often rise in proportion to the inflation rate. One notable exception is the U.S. federal tax rate, which rises out of proportion to everything.

I.R.R. "Internal rate of return." The implied rate of return of an investment, assuming complete reinvestment of cash flows. Not to be confused with L.I.R.R., the Long Island Rail Road, which has an I.R.R. of less than zero.

I.T.C. "Investment tax credit." A 10 percent tax break (based on purchase price of equipment) instituted by Congress in the early 1960s to spur capital investment by corporations.

K.S.F. "Key success factor." Another all-purpose term used by M.B.A.'s to summarize or simplify the things that make an operation or person effective. The K.S.F. for *Penthouse* magazine, for example, is that publication's artistic integrity.

Learning Curve A theoretical curve describing the reduction in production cost achieved by a company as it gains experience in making a product. First publicized by consulting firms, the term has now been adapted for popular use, as in "When I was a freshman in college it took me three hours to get through the Sunday *Times.* Now I can skim it in ten minutes, so I guess I'm coming down the learning curve."

Leverage 1. A measurement of the amount of money a company or person borrows relative to its net worth. Thus, a company with $50 million in net worth and $100 million of debt is using two-to-one *leverage.* 2. A term used by M.B.A.'s in nonfinancial contexts, such as "My two assistants really leverage my time." 3. A favorite term of panhandlers on Wall Street.

Liquidation Generally, the disposal of assets through sale or abandonment. In certain "family-controlled" industries, however (see the chapter on "Corporate Strategy"), it refers to the disposal of competing management personnel.

LTD 1. "Long-term debt." 2. Shorthand for "limited," the British term for "incorporated." 3. A Ford sedan once favored by aspiring middle managers.

Management The art of getting other people to do all the work.

Marginal Another all-purpose word, borrowed by business from economics. Marginal cost, for example, is the cost incurred if one additional unit of a good is produced. Also used as a modifier in "marginal tax rate," "marginal revenue," "marginal utility," and "marginal elements of society."

Maturity 1. The date on which bonds or bank loans become due and payable. 2. The late phase of a product or company when growth in sales has slowed (see the "Marketing" chapter). 3. A quality of character, the lack of which is often displayed by executives haggling over the location of their office parking spaces.

M.B.A. Acronym for several different—but related —terms: 1. Master of Business Administration. 2. Master Bull Artist. 3. Master of Blind Ambition.

M.B.O. "Management by objective." The concept of rewarding executives solely on their ability to meet or exceed specific corporate goals. One of the most fashionable organizational behavior concepts of the late 1960s, it has fallen into disfavor for being too inflexible. The institution of M.B.O. systems in major corporations provided the majority of consulting income to O.B. specialists during the 1960s. The removal of M.B.O. systems from major corporations provided the majority of consulting income to O.B. specialists during the 1970s.

Missionary Selling Preaching product or service attributes to the non-believing, heathen buyer (see *Cannibalization*).

BARNYARD FINANCE
Important business
creatures to recognize

Bear	A speculator who thinks the stock market is headed south.
Bull	A wildly optimistic speculator who thinks the stock market is going up.
Cash Cow	A no-growth investment that still gives milk (that is, good dividends).
Dog	A stock with no sex appeal.
Pig	As in "Bulls and Bears make money, but Pigs never do."
Steer	A Bull who was cut down to size by one too many market reverses.

Moody's A bond-rating service (see *S & P*).

Mullet A naive but wealthy investor, the constant mark of stockbrokers and shady tax-shelter salesmen. Unlike most investors, mullets eagerly risk their wealth on get-rich-quick schemes they fail to understand and which have no hope of making it past the IRS. Synonyms: doctor, dentist.

Mushroom Theory Refers to the way most corporate research and de-velopment (see *R & D*) operations are run. The theory states that you put a bunch of guys in a dark room, dump a big pile of manure on them, and see if anything useful comes up.

Mutual Fund A vehicle for investing in diverse stock-market portfolios that are professionally mismanaged.

N.P.V. "Net present value." The value of projected "cash flows" returned by an investment, *discounted* back to the present. For example, the N.P.V. of the $300-a-week pension you expect to get twenty years from now, discounted back to the present at current inflation rates, is worth about enough to buy you a hot pastrami sandwich.

Number Crunching Spending late nights working out numbers on a calculator. Recently recognized as the cause of one of business's most debilitating diseases, the formation of painful calluses on an executive's calculator finger that are detrimental to his tennis swing.

O.P.I.C. Overseas Private Investment Corporation. A quasi-public agency of the U.S. government that insures investments made overseas by U.S. corporations, protecting them from seizure by Third World nations who are members of O.P.*E*.C.

O.P.M. "Other people's money." Also, the name of a now-bankrupt computer-leasing firm that made

maximum use of O.P.M. by defrauding people into lending it to them.

Opportunity Cost The implicit cost of forgoing an opportunity because you or your capital is busy elsewhere. Example: the two years of salary forgone while you languish in business school.

O.T.C. "Over the counter." A term for stock not listed on the New York or American Stock exchanges. Not to be confused with O.T.T. ("over the transom"), O.T.L. ("out to lunch"), or U.T.T. ("under the table").

Overhead The fixed, unavoidable costs of operating a business. Examples include the cost of manufacturing facilities for an industrial company, the salary of your boss, the corporate jet, the president's limousine. Revenue to support these and other essentials is raised through the levy of overhead contribution taxes on the profitable operating divisions of the company.

Par 1. The stated guaranteed liquidation value of a share of common stock; thus, "a stock with par value of $1." 2. An *acceptably good* performance, as in "The comptroller's performance was up to par this year." 3. In golf, a score of one stroke per hole more than your client.

Parent Company A holding company that owns a controlling interest in another company (usually known as a subsidiary). Recent flurries of acquisitions and rapid divestitures of subsidiaries (see the "Finance" chapter) make many of these holding companies more like foster parents than natural ones.

Play A way of investing in a particular type of market action, be it interest rate fluctuations, natural resources, or technological breakthroughs. For example, Marvin Davis's purchase of Twentieth Century-Fox for its $500 million worth of Hollywood backlots was a "real estate play." For most people, investing in commodity futures is a "sucker play."

P.R. "Public relations." A profession that publicizes the good things about a company and glosses over the rough spots, such as Three Mile Island, Love Canal, the Ford Pinto, or Firestone 500's.

Price Umbrella Shelter provided to a small company when a competitor who owns most of the market sets prices abnormally high. When the FCC sets high long-distance telephone rates for AT&T to subsidize local calling, it provides a price umbrella, under which smaller long-distance competitors like MCI and Sprint can profitably huddle while undercutting AT&T's prices.

Profit 1. The difference between cost and sales price. 2. The bottom line. 3. A four-letter word to people who can't count.

Psychological Contract The *unwritten* understanding between employee and employer, as in "Asking me to pick up your dry cleaning is not only not in my job description, it's a violation of my psychological contract!"

R & D "Research and development." Expenditures on new ideas or future products that a company makes in order to upgrade their products in the future. Often compared to elephants making love: there's a lot of trumpeting and writhing in the beginning, but nothing comes of it for at least twenty-seven months (see *Mushroom Theory*).

Reactive/Proactive A *reactive* executive responds to problems after they happen, but a *proactive* one anticipates them. Executives who use this phrase inevitably characterize themselves as proactive.

Recession / Depression Recession is when your neighbor loses his job; depression is when *you* lose yours. These eco-nomic downturns are very difficult to forecast, but sophisticated econometric modeling houses like Data Resources and Chase Econometrics have successfully predicted fourteen of the last three recessions.

Retrofit 1. Modernizing previously installed plant or equipment in order to bring it into compliance with updated environmental standards or technical conditions. Example: adding pollution control scrubbers to factory smokestacks. 2. Used informally in business to describe *any* modification, as in "If I have another piece of cake, I'll have to get my suits retrofitted."

Reverse Polish Notation A way of expressing mathematical calculations used only by Nobel Prize–winning mathematicians and hot-shot executives who have mastered their Hewlett-Packard calculators.

Risk/Return The generally positive relationship between the returns from an investment and the risk involved in making it. Translation: No guts, no glory.

ROI "Return on investment." In French, the word *roi* means "king," but in American business, the acronym ROI *is* king. Return on investment is the driving criterion behind most business decisions, as it expresses the amount of profitable bang a company can expect to get back for each invested buck.

S & P Standard & Poor's. A bond and stock rating service (see *Moody's*).

Sale/Leaseback An arrangement whereby one company sells assets to another company, then leases them back. Purposes: (a) to raise quick cash; (b) to transfer tax benefits like depreciation to a company that has income to deduct them from.

Scenario A set of imagined sequences of events that provide the context in which a business decision

is made. Scenarios always come in sets of threes: best case, worst case, and just in case.

S.E.C. Securities and Exchange Commission. Formed by Congress to regulate the stock market in the wake of the Great Crash of 1929. First commissioner: Joseph P. Kennedy (patriarch of the Kennedy clan), who made millions manipulating stock prices when it was still legal, and then closed the door behind him.

Secondary Market An exchange or market where previously owned assets—stocks, bonds, or mortgages—are traded. Examples: the New York Stock Exchange, the Pacific Stock Exchange, the corner singles bar.

Sensitivity 1. The degree to which an action will affect a given measure of performance, as in "Our profit is very sensitive to market share." 2. *(archaic)* The ability of a manager to get in tune with his associates.

Short-term Optimizer A term used to describe executives who make decisions with an eye on the next quarter's financial statements rather than the long-term good of the company. Antonym of big-picture thinker. Sometimes used as synonym for M.B.A.

S.O.B. "Son of Boss."

Synergy A critical buzzword. See the "Finance" chapter for a detailed description.

System Another A.P.B. (all-purpose buzzword) used to modify every imaginable aspect of business or the economy. Thus, financial system, accounting system, monetary system, distribution system, political system, production system, The System. Madison Avenue types have recognized a good buzzword when they hear it; thus, a car wax with buffing pad becomes "a complete car care system."

Upstream / Downstream Describes the acquisition by a business of related manufacturing or marketing capabilities. If Kodak were to buy a chain of retail stores to sell its film, it would be "integrating *downstream.*" When, earlier in this century, Kodak raised horses in order to process them into gelatin for film manufacture, that was "integrating *upstream.*"

THE FORMULA FOR SUCCESS

$$\text{Success} = \left[A\left(\frac{R \times C^2}{E}\right) + P(B)^3 + G \right]^{L} + W$$

Key:

A = Ambition
B = Buzzword proficiency
C = Chutzpah
E = Excessive education (M.B.A.)
G = Golf handicap
L = Luck
P = Power Accessories
R = Resume expansion
W = Work

8

THE FORMULA
FOR SUCCESS